lonely planet

POCKET

HOBART

TOP EXPERIENCES · LOCAL LIFE

T0022839

CHARLES RAWLINGS-WAY

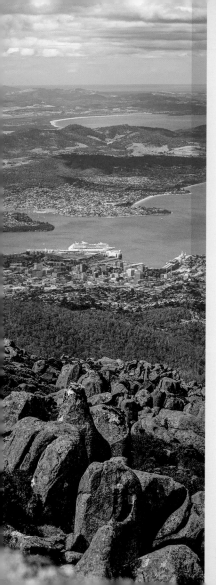

Contents

Plan Your Trip   4

Hobart from kunanyi/Mt Wellington (p136)
YEVGEN BELICH/SHUTTERSTOCK ©

Explore Hobart 37

Worth a Trip

Special Features

Survival Guide 140

COVID-19

We have rechecked every business in this book before publication to ensure that it is still open after the COVID-19 outbreak. However, the economic and social impacts of COVID-19 will continue to be felt long after the outbreak has been contained, and many businesses, services and events referenced in this guide may experience ongoing restrictions. Some businesses may be temporarily closed, have changed their opening hours and services, or require bookings; some unfortunately could have closed permanently. We suggest you check with venues before visiting for the latest information.

Top Experiences

Experience the Extraordinary MONA
Show-stopping force of culture. **p102**

IMAGE COURTESY OF THE ARTIST AND MONA MUSEUM OF OLD AND NEW ART, HOBART, TASMANIA, AUSTRALIA/JESSE HUNNIFORD ©

Wander Through Salamanca Place

Bars, cafes, restaurants and galleries. **p56**

Explore Maritime History at Battery Point
Hobart's first suburb. **p108**

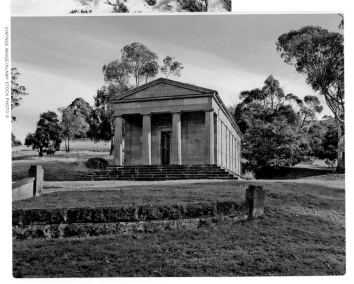

Climb kunanyi/ Mt Wellington

Best views in the business. **p136**

Discover Trendy North Hobart

The city's bohemian heart- and art-land. **p86**

Tour the Cascade Brewery

A real Hobart 'must do'. **p128**

DOUGLAS CLIFF/SHUTTERSTOCK ©

SUE BURTON PHOTOGRAPHY/SHUTTERSTOCK ©

Witness History at the Cascades Female Factory Historic Site

Where Hobart's female convicts were incarcerated. **p132**

Explore the Tasmanian Museum & Art Gallery

Extensive collection of paintings and relics. **p60**

Dining Out

Eating in Hobart is one of the true pleasures of any visit down south. Local 'Mod Oz' (Modern Australian) restaurateurs are wide awake to southern Tasmania's excellent produce, and are doing good things with it in the city's kitchens. The cafe and coffee scenes here, too, will keep you sustained, while seafood and pub-grub offerings are also reliably good.

Dining Destinations

Hobart's city centre proffers some excellent cafes and rapid-fire lunch venues, but when the sun sinks behind the mountain, there's not a whole lot going on here (with some notable exceptions). Instead, head for the waterfront and Salamanca Place, the epicentre of the city's culinary scene, where there's quality seafood everywhere you look.

Battery Point's Hampden Rd cafes and restaurants are always worth a look, while Elizabeth St in North Hobart (aka 'NoHo') has evolved into a diverse collection of cosmopolitan eateries: Indian, Asian, Mexican, cafes, patisseries, pubs...

The Sandy Bay food scene is also bubbling along nicely (any suggestions for a cool nickname?).

Dinner Time?

Hobartians are big on breakfast and dinner, but lunch is something that sometimes morphs intro brunch or is squeezed in between other commitments. That said, a cafe breakfast isn't a daily event here – more of a weekend treat. A takeaway coffee is, however, a daily necessity for many folks.

It's probably something to do with chilly southern weather, but dinner happens early in Hobart: 6pm is a very reasonable hour to eat, and don't expect to arrive anywhere after 8.30pm and get a table.

THREEBEANIES/SHUTTERSTOCK ©

Best Cafes

Jackman & McRoss This iconic Battery Point cafe is still going strong. Great staff and creative baking. (pictured; p118)

Sweet Envy As if the Elizabeth St strip in North Hobart wasn't sweet enough! Divine sweet treats. (p95)

Retro Cafe A pioneering Salamanca Place cafe in a prime spot for people watching. (p72)

Pilgrim Coffee Progressive pilgrim sets the pace in Hobart's downtown coffee scene. (p48)

Best Seafood & Steak

Flippers Super-fresh seafood to go, down on the waterfront. (p73)

Fish Frenzy Family-focussed seafood diner on the waterfront, with an eternally buzzy vibe. (p74)

Blue Eye High-end seafood at the far end of Salamanca Place. (p78)

Best Upmarket Dining

Don Camillo One of Hobart's first restaurants is still one of the best: superb

Italian offerings in Sandy Bay. (p123)

Templo Templo sets the tempo on an unremarkable street, with entirely remarkable eats. (p48)

Aloft The best views in town from atop the Brook St Pier. (p77)

Frank Frankly fabulous South American–inspired cuisine down on the waterfront. (p77)

> ### Worth a Trip
>
> About 3km north of the city centre, the stylish, light-filled **Cornelian Bay Boat House** (p99) restaurant-bar occupies a converted beach pavilion. The highly evolved menu features quality local produce, delivered with super service.

Bar Open

Hobart's younger drinkers are 10,000 leagues removed from the rum-addled whalers of the past, but the general intentions remain true – drink a bit, relax a lot, and maybe get lucky and take someone home. Salamanca Place, the waterfront and North Hobart are the main drinking and nocturnal hubs.

Pubs

Hobart once had so many pubs it was hard to walk more than a few hundred metres without being tempted into one for a quick ale. These days a lot of them around the city centre have closed (or been turned into backpacker hostels), with new craft-beer, whisky and cocktail bars the flavour of the decade. But you can still sniff out a few endearing old boozers here and there if you know where to look. Most pubs offer hefty traditional lunches from noon to 2pm, and dinners from 6pm to 8pm (young families get in early), plus open fires in the winter and occasional live tunes.

Bars

In a town renowned for drinking, it was just a matter of time before traditional all-things-to-all-people pubs gave way to more specialised booze rooms, dabbling in the dark arts of whisky, wine, cocktails and craft beers. These days there are plenty of hip little places where you can indulge your particular liquid whims, from dedicated wine bars to an emerging crew of craft-beer bars and moody outlets for fine Tasmanian whisky.

Best Traditional Pubs

Hope & Anchor Australia's oldest pub? Take up the discussion with the bar staff. (pictured; p51)

Shipwright's Arms Hotel Marvellously old-school backstreet pub in Battery Point. (p124)

WILLIAM CARAM/ALAMY STOCK PHOTO ©

New Sydney Hotel The best watering hole in the city centre has open fires, excellent food and interesting beers. (p50)

Best Wine, Whisky & Cocktails

Glass House The newest cocktail bar in town, with unbeatable river views and stylin' staff. (p78)

Willing Bros Uncork (or unscrew) a bottle of something luscious in North Hobart. (p100)

T-42° Enduring waterside classiness in the Elizabeth St Pier. (p79)

Grape Local, mainland and imported wines line the walls in this charming little cave. (p80)

Best Craft-Beer Bars

The Winston Rootsy North Hobart epicentre for all things cold and crafty. (p99)

Preachers A raffish backstreet Battery Point brew bar full of student types...and a ghost! (p124)

Hobart Brewing Company Roll up, roll up: waterfront beers in the emerging Macquarie Point precinct. (p78)

T-Bone Brewing Co Nifty North Hobart brew-bar just south of the main Elizabeth St strip. (p99)

Worth a Trip

Almost within eyeshot of the famous old Cascade Brewery just around the corner, the **Cascade Hotel** (p125) in South Hobart has been pouring the local product since 1846. These days it's a reliable locals' hangout with decent pub food (famously good steaks) and occasional live music, including free-wheeling jazz jams every Wednesday night.

Treasure Hunt

No one has ever said, 'I'm off to Hobart with the express purpose of doing some serious shopping – can't wait!'. That said, there are some fabulous markets here, plus quirky city shops, purveyors of fine food and drink, quality bookshops, outdoor stores aplenty, and some brilliant galleries around Salamanca Place.

Top Tips

Hiking, camping, fishing and skiing is big business here: outdoors shops cluster around the Elizabeth St/Bathurst St intersection, or head to Kathmandu in Salamanca Square.

Hobart is chilly in winter (and, truth be told, at times in spring, autumn and summer): it follows that the bookshops here are pretty good! Get yourself something good to leaf through by an open fire.

Best Bookshops

Fullers Bookshop Hobart's best bookshop maintains a high literary tone, with launches, readings and a cool cafe. (p52)

Hobart Book Shop Nooked in behind Salamanca Place, with a terrific Tasmanian section. (p83)

Tasmanian Map Centre Bushwalking map or a Lonely Planet travel guide, anyone? (p53)

State Cinema Bookstore Next to North Hobart's brilliant art-house cinema, with a predictably arty/noir bent. (p101)

Best Art & Antiques

Despard Gallery Hip Battery Point gallery offerings, with especially beautiful canvasses. (p126)

Salamanca Arts Centre Arts co-op in the Salamanca Place warehouses, with around 75 vendors. (p70)

Handmark Gallery From delicate to bold: 100% Tasmanian ceramics, glass, woodwork and jewellery. (p82)

Art Mob Gorgeous hyper-coloured Aboriginal art from around the country. (p83)

LEISA TYLER/GETTY IMAGES ©

Best Speciality Shops

Fullers Bookshop Time is meaningless in Hobart's best bookshop: step inside then emerge pleasantly bewildered, three hours later. (p52)

Cool Wine The best of Tasmania's super cool-climate wines – and beer, whisky, gin, cider... (p41)

Wursthaus Kitchen Stock up on gourmet goodies at this excellent deli, just off Salamanca Place. (p82)

Tommy Gun Records Thumb through racks of vinyl and tune in to the sounds of the city. (p41)

State Cinema Bookstore Browse arty titles adjacent to North Hobart's State Cinema. (p101)

Handmark Gallery Hand-made, 100% Tasmanian arts and crafts on Salamanca Place: Handmark sets the benchmark. (p82)

Kathmandu Gear-up for your imminent Tasmanian wilderness adventure. (p83)

Best Markets

Salamanca Market Hobart's famous street market happens every Saturday morning, rain or shine. (pictured; p81)

Farm Gate Market Upstart Sunday-morning food-and-drink market on Bathurst St in the city. (p47)

Street Eats @ Franko Ebullient Friday-night food, drinks and entertainment at Franklin Sq in the city centre. (p47)

Historic Atmosphere

Hobart is endowed with more than its fair share of impressive (and at times, downright cute) historic buildings, many built with local sandstone that takes on a warm glow in Tasmania's soft southern light. Visiting Hobart's museums and walking around the city, the waterfront and Battery Point, it's easy to conjure up visions of days gone by.

Heritage Buildings

Hobart's amazing cache of well-cured old buildings makes it exceptional among Australian cities. There are more than 90 buildings classified by the National Trust here – 60 of them are on Macquarie and Davey Sts alone. The intersection of these streets features a gorgeous heritage sandstone edifice on each corner – the only instance of this in Australia – including the austere St David's Cathedral. Salamanca Place is of course

a must-see; also worth a look is the 1864 Town Hall on Macquarie St – duck inside the lobby and have a look around.

Domestic Architecture

Hobart has been both cursed and blessed by Tasmania's stop-start economy. These days things are very much in the 'start' category, but often in the past local business sentiment has been catatonic at best. This economic lethargy, combined with a general lack of wealth in society, has

been a blessing for Hobart's old houses: there just hasn't been enough money around to bulldoze old homes and build new ones. The net result? Hobart's stock of domestic architecture is now beautifully preserved. Georgian, Victorian, Edwardian, Federation, modern, mid-century...drive around the suburbs and play 'Name That Architectural Style'.

Best Museums & Historic Sights

Cascades Female Factory Historic Site Hobart's female convicts lived,

LKONYA/SHUTTERSTOCK ©

worked and died at this haunting South Hobart site. (p132)

Cascade Brewery It's not just about beer: the brewery itself is an imposing hark-back to old-time Hobart. (p128)

Tasmanian Museum & Art Gallery Aboriginal history, colonial heritage and the demise of the thylacine: just part of TMAG's broad historical remit. (p60)

Narryna Heritage Museum A window into the domestic lives of Hobart's colonial families. (pictured; p117)

Penitentiary Chapel Historic Site This spooky old chapel and prison complex on the city fringe is a disquieting place. (p45)

Best Historic Vibes

Battery Point Take a time-travelling stroll around the streets of Battery Point, Hobart's first neighbourhood. (p108)

Salamanca Place The marvellous old stone ware-houses along Salamanca Place are utterly photogenic. (p56)

Henry Jones Art Hotel Built inside an old warehouse on Hunter St, this former jam factory is now an atmospheric boutique hotel. (p65)

Hope & Anchor Thirsty? Sit at the bar of Australia's oldest pub and soak up the vibes. (p51)

Worth a Trip

Drive out to the historic town of **Richmond** (population 1610), straddling the Coal River 27km northeast of Hobart. Once a strategic military post and convict station, the town is riddled with 19th-century buildings. There's also the day-trip bonus of the Coal River Valley wineries are en route.

Showtime

Some Hobartians come home in the evening, open a beer and sit and watch the sun set behind kunanyi/Mt Wellington – what more entertainment do you need? A bit of live music, perhaps: Hobart is host to a clutch of good live-music pubs and a classical concert hall. The theatre scene simmers along here, too, and there are some top-notch sporting events to admire.

Live Music

Hobart is big on drinking, and big on providing a live-music soundtrack to which you may drink. The bands that play the pub circuit here have long been mired in a cover-version cycle of doomed creativity – and compared to Melbourne or even Adelaide they still are. But the originals scene here is slowly gaining traction, and most nights of the week now you can hear something new and vaguely rockin'.

The live jazz scene here is much smaller, little trios and quartets sometimes popping up at waterfront bars (try Grape, IXL Long Bar or the Salamanca Whisky Bar). On the classical front, the Tasmanian Symphony Orchestra plays at the waterfront Federation Concert Hall.

Spectator Sports

Like to watch? In winter you can catch live Australian Football League (AFL; www.afl.com.au) games at Blundstone Arena in Bellerive on Hobart's eastern shore, with international and state cricket gracing the same venue in summer. Tennis fans look forward to the annual **Hobart International** (www.hobartinternational.com.au; ◷ Jan) womens' pro tournament every January (a prelude to the Australian Open in Melbourne).

Best Cinema

State Cinema A cornerstone of Hobart's artistic life, the art-house State has eight screens, a cafe-bar and a bookshop. (p101)

MONA MONA has its very own cinema called Cinemona, screening arty recent releases and classics. (p102)

DANIEL POCKETT - CA/GETTY IMAGES ©

Best Live Music

Republic Bar & Café
Original rock, blues and folk acts most nights, both local and touring. (p101)

Brisbane Hotel Offbeat metal, punk, hip-hip and alt-rock in a city boozer that's been here forever. (p51)

Irish Murphy's Waterside Irish predictability, but with entertaining covers acts, open-mic nights and lots of originals. (p81)

Federation Concert Hall Highbrow classical on the waterfront, courtesy of the Tasmanian Symphony Orchestra. (p81)

IXL Long Bar Regular live jazz in the old Hunter St warehouses. (p79)

Best Theatre

Theatre Royal Australia's oldest theatre (1834) still has its old boards and actors treading on them. (p43)

Peacock Theatre An engaging programme of theatre, dance, music and film in a cute little theatre off Salamanca Place. (p81)

Playhouse Theatre Long-running drama hub on Bathurst St in the city, producing musicals aplenty. (p51)

Worth a Trip

Hobart's home of cricket and football is **Blundstone Arena** (pictured; Bellerive Oval; 📍tickets 13 28 49, tours 03-6282 0400; www.blundstonearena. com.au; 15 Derwent St, Bellerive; tours adult/chld $15/5; ⏱tours 10am Tue & Wed, 1pm Thu). The **North Melbourne Kangaroos AFL football club** (www.afl.com.au) plays some home games here; international test, one-day and T20 cricket matches also pull crowds.

Parks, Gardens & Viewpoints

Hobart isn't what you'd call a 'leafy city'; the wilderness was the enemy in the 1800s. The flip-side of this clear-felling attitude is that there are some beautiful, manicured parks and gardens (reproducing old England was conceptually easier for the colonists to handle). There are also some terrific vantage points around town.

Points of View

Hobart is so scenic, it's almost a prerequisite for houses to have a view of some sort: the river, the mountain, maybe both. With the notable exception of Sydney, most mainland Australian cities are aesthetically impoverished by comparison. Formal vantage points with pay-per-view binoculars, hotdog vans and oceans of car parking don't exist here: it's more a case of just driving around and seeing what you can see. There are views everywhere!

You won't find it in any tourist brochures, but for a classic view of Hobart and the Derwent River with the hulking mass of kunanyi/ Mt Wellington in the background, drive up to the local-secret lookout atop Rosy Hill on Hobart's eastern shore. The local council thoughtfully lops the tops off any trees that dare impede the view. To get here, cross the Tasman Bridge, head for Rosny, turn right at the lights onto Riawena Rd and follow the signs.

Best Parks & Gardens

Royal Tasmanian Botanical Gardens Fourteen gorgeous hectares of immaculate lawns, exotic plant collections, greenhouses, fountains and ancient trees, some dating back to the late 1800s. (pictured; p93)

Princes Park Where once stood Battery Point's namesake gun battery is now this lovely park, with a fab kids' playground and lawns sloping down towards the river.

Cenotaph The Cenotaph itself is a towering war memorial, but the lawns surrounding it give Hobartians a much needed sense of wide-open space. (p94)

EDEN NGUYEN/SHUTTERSTOCK ©

Queen's Domain Part of the Queen's Domain – the bulky hillock just to the north of the city – is consumed by Glebe, a sunny little suburb. The rest is semi-wilderness, cloaked in casuarinas, eucalypts and grasslands. (p93)

Napoleon St Playground This trim little park in Battery Point has a sunny patch of lawn for mum and dad to snooze on while the kids run amok. (p113)

Best Viewpoints

kunanyi/Mt Wellington There's no denying kunanyi – the big mountain is a key component of daily life in Hobart. And even if you drive half-way up Pinnacle Rd, the views over the city and beyond are astonishing. (p136)

Victoria Dock For a picture-postcard view of Hobart, wander over to the north side of Victoria Dock on the waterfront and look back towards the city: fishing boats, office blocks and the marvellous mountain. (p65)

Roaring 40s Kayaking Grab an eyeful of Battery Point and the waterfront from the river on these excellent guided kayak paddles. (p118)

MONA ferry Don't bother driving to MONA: catch the ferry instead. Sip champagne in the 'Posh Pit' and assess the city and northern suburbs from the water. (p103)

Worth a Trip

kunanyi/Mt Wellington is irrefutably big, but if the summit is clouded over and you're still looking for a view, the old semaphore station atop **Mt Nelson** (352m; p113) provides immaculate views over Hobart and the Derwent River. Drive up Davey St from the city, take the Southern Outlet towards Kingston and turn left at the top of the hill – or use local buses 457, 458 and X58.

Museums

Hobart is a really old town as far as white Australian history goes – only Sydney predates it. It follows, then, that the museums here are chock-full of interesting old things. And of course, Aboriginal history in the Hobart area goes back many tens of thousands of years – check out the Tasmanian Museum & Art Gallery for some engaging indigenous insights.

JOYCE MAR/SHUTTERSTOCK ©

Reading History

In Hobart, history lives in the architecture, the streets and the landscape. Museums offer a mainline to the past, but some pre-trip reading will get your in the mood:

○ *In Search of Hobart* (Peter Timms; 2009) Part social history, part contemporary critique.

○ *Thylacine* (David Owen; 2003) A poignant recounting of the demise of the Tasmanian tiger.

Best Museums

MONA Much more than just a museum, MONA is an ethos, a philosophy, a way of life! Allow a full day here (at least): built-in eating and drinking venues will keep you fuelled up. (p102)

Tasmanian Museum & Art Gallery 'TMAG' has really lifted its game in recent years. This rather amazing collection of old buildings is now a must-visit Hobart experience. (pictured; p60)

Maritime Museum of Tasmania Hobart and the sea are locked together for eternity. What the sea wants, the sea shall have... (p70)

Mawson's Huts Replica Museum See how the intrepid Sir Douglas Mawson coped with the cold of Antarctica in 1911. (p70)

Narynna Heritage Museum Hobart domestic life in colonial times is perfectly preserved at Narynna, in Battery Point. (p117)

Markree House Museum Markree House lifts the lid on Hobart between the wars (not quite mid-century modern, but almost as hip). (p45)

Allport Library & Museum of Fine Arts Adjunct to the State Library and beautifully bookish, this excellent little city museum is a trove of wonderful art. (p43)

Activities

Surf beaches, kunanyi/Mt Wellington, the Derwent River and, of course, Tasmania's world-famous wilderness areas are all within easy reach of Hobart. Cycling, mountain biking and bushwalking are de rigueur here: see the Greater Hobart Trails website (www.greaterhobarttrails.com.au) for details on dozens of options around the city.

SLOW WALKER/SHUTTERSTOCK ©

Swimming & Surfing

Hobart's city beaches look inviting, especially at Bellerive and Sandy Bay, but the water can get a bit soupy. For a safe, clean swim, you'll be better off heading further south to the beaches at **Kingston** and **Blackmans Bay**. Or smash out some laps at the Hobart Aquatic Centre.

The most reliable local surfing spots near Hobart are **Clifton Beach** (pictured) and **Goats Beach**, en route to South Arm – about 30km and 35km from Hobart respectively. Note that Goats is unpatrolled and has a strong longshore drift.

Best Activities

Mt Wellington Descent Fly down Mt Wellington on a mountain bike. (p137)

Roaring 40s Kayaking Paddle the Battery Point foreshore, Hobart wharves and beyond. (p118)

kunanyi/Mt Wellington Tackle a steep mountainside track on Hobart's resident peak. (p136)

Hobart Bike Hire Get two wheels underneath you and explore the city, or pedal the 20km north to MONA along a Intercity Cycleway. (p71)

Hobart Aquatic Centre Cool off with a splash at Hobart's excellent swim centre. (p94)

Top Tips

Hobart isn't big on bike lanes, but there's a terrific cycling path running from the Cenotaph near the waterfront to MONA, following an old railway line. It's called the **Intercity Cycleway**, and is about 20km one-way; see www.greaterhobarttrails.com.au/track/intercity-cycleway for details.

Tours

Taking a guided tour is a terrific way to get under Hobart's skin, be it with a historic, foodie, boozy or active focus. And if you don't have your own transport, taking a tour is the only way to access some key sights in and around Hobart, including kunanyi/ Mt Wellington.

JEJIM/SHUTTERSTOCK ©

Top Tips

River cruises (including the ferry to MONA) set sail from the Hobart waterfront.

Most bus tours depart from the Hobart Visitor Information Centre at the lower end of Elizabeth St.

Most tours run daily during summer (December to February), but schedules and prices vary with the season and demand.

Best Sightseeing

Pennicott Wilderness Journeys Outstanding boat trips to some gorgeous southern coastal spots. (p70)

Red Decker If you're short on time, this big red hop-on/ hop-off bus is the way to see the sights. (pictured; p72)

Tours Tasmania Day trips around Hobart and a trip up kunanyi/Mt Wellington. (p72)

Hobart Historic Tours Boat tours on the river. (p46)

Best Food & Drink Tours

Gourmania Excellent walking tours around Hobart and Salamanca Place, stopping to taste as often as possible. (p71)

Drink Tasmania Whisky, wine, beer and cider: day trips from the waterfront to sample the best drops. (p71)

Best Walking Tours

Hobart Historic Tours Entertaining strolls around the old town and Battery Point. Pub tours also available. (p46)

Ghost Tours of Hobart & Battery Point There are more than a few skeletons rattling in Hobart's closet. (p118)

Hobart Comedy Tours Walk around Franklin Sq in the city centre and have a laugh at Hobart's expense.

Festivals

XAVIER HOENNER/SHUTTERSTOCK ©

Best in Summer

Taste of Tasmania On either side of New Year's Eve, this week-long harbourside event is a celebration of Tassie's gastronomic prowess. The seafood, wines and cheeses are predictably fab, or branch out into mushrooms, truffles, raspberries... Stalls are a who's-who of the Hobart restaurant scene. Live music, too. Just brilliant. (p74)

Hobart International As a prelude to the Australian Open tennis championship in Melbourne later in January, the Hobart International draws plenty of big-name players (just the ladies) for a week-long tournament. (p18)

Sydney to Hobart Yacht Race Maxi-yachts competing in the world's most gruelling open-ocean race start arriving in Hobart around 29 December – just in time for New Year's Eve! (Yachties sure can party.) (p74)

MONA FOMA MONA's Festival of Music & Arts is a highlight of Hobart's busy January party schedule. Classy acts of all genres and persuasions. (p105)

Best in Winter

Dark MOFO This noir little number broods in the low light of June's winter solstice. Expect edgy performances, epic installations, poetry, film, bonfires, red wine and feasting, all mainlining Tasmania's gothic blood flow. (pictured; p105)

For Free

There are plenty of free markets and indoor/outdoor activities around Hobart that won't shred the contents of your wallet. Our best advice is to sight-see under your own steam: it's a compact town by Australian standards, with the city centre, waterfront, Salamanca Place and Battery Point all withing striding distance of one another. Even North Hobart is walkable.

ANDREW BALCOMBE/SHUTTERSTOCK ©

Best Outdoors

Royal Tasmanian Botanical Gardens We're not sure that Queen Liz comes here too often, but these lovely gardens are a top spot for a stroll. (p93)

kunanyi/Mt Wellington 'The mountain' is free but delivers in spades: drive to the summit, scan the far horizons, maybe throw a few snowballs... (pictured; p136)

Waterfront Ship-spotters rejoice! Hobart's harbour is a busy hub of comings and goings: yachts, fishing boats, cruise ships, Antarctic supply vessels...

Battery Point Get a dose of Hobart history with a self-guided wander around this super-charming historic enclave. (p108)

Best Indoors

Tasmanian Museum & Art Gallery TMAG is free to all comers – what a noble piece of state government magnanimity! (p60)

Hobart Real Tennis Club Visit this historic hall on Davey St and watch some free 'real' tennis (like the outdoor version, but with zany quirks). (p43)

Parliament House Tours of Hobart's stately waterfront Parliament House are free (not when parliament is sitting, unfortunately). (p67)

Gasworks Cellar Door Wander through the rooms of this interesting wine centre and learn all about Tasmania's booming booze industry. (p43)

Best Markets

Salamanca Market Hobart's famous street market is a commercial free-for-all. Don't even think about doing anything else on a Saturday morning. (p81)

Farm Gate Market You'll probably end up buying some food here (thus it's not technically free), but you can't put a price on atmosphere and good vibes. (p47)

Street Eats @ Franko Tune in to some free live music at this engaging Friday-night food mart in Franklin Sq. (p47)

Under the Radar

Salamanca Place overrun with tourists? Can't get a seat in that seafood restaurant you've had your eye on? Too many elbows at the bar? Take time out from Hobart's busy scenes and explore the city's beach suburbs: take a chilly dip, settle into a cafe for the afternoon, or just snooze on the sand and forget about where you have to be tomorrow.

TOM JASTRAM/SHUTTERSTOCK ©

Best Beach 'Burbs

Seven Mile Beach (pictured) Out near the Hobart Airport, 15km east of Hobart, is this brilliant, safe swimming beach backed by shacks, a corner store and pine-punctured dunes, plus an oyster farm nearby.

Taroona 10km south of Hobart you'll find the laid-back residential beach suburb Taroona. The pub here may have closed, but Hinsby Beach, alongside the lofty Alum Cliffs, remains one of the best spots in town for a swim. There's also excellent cafe occupying the old petrol station here.

Kingston Sprawling Kingston, 12km south of Hobart, is a booming outer suburb. Kingston Beach here is great for a swim on a sunny afternoon, and there are some fab places to eat and drink along the waterfront. Behind the sailing club at the beach's southern end is a track leading to Boronia Beach, a secret little swimming cove.

Blackmans Bay About 3km south of Kingston, Blackmans Bay has a safe-swimming beach and a blowhole. The water is usually cold, and there's rarely any surf...but it sure is pretty! If you wander around the cliff base near the blowhole, you'll find a local-secret swimming gulch, with waves surging in and out of a deep channel.

For Kids

Hobart is an outdoorsy kinda town, and despite its rep for being cold (yes, it is), it's the second driest capital city in Australia. There's lots to do that's free, good museums for when it does rain, and plenty of active things to do around town.

WILLOWTREEHOUSE/SHUTTERSTOCK ©

Best Entertainment

Rektango The free Friday-night Rektango music event in the courtyard at the Salamanca Arts Centre is a family-friendly affair: wear your dancin' shoes. (p59)

Salamanca Market The street performers, buskers and visual smorgasbord of Saturday's Salamanca Market captivate kids of all ages. (pictured; p81)

Waterfront There's always something going on down on the Hobart waterfront – fishing boats chugging in and out of Victoria Dock, yachts tacking in Sullivans Cove – and you can feed the tribe on a budget at the floating fish punts on Constitution Dock (seagulls guaranteed).

Best Rainy-day Distractions

Tasmanian Museum & Art Gallery Check out some Aboriginal history, get the low-down on the elusive Tasmanian tiger and ogle some shiny stones – what's not to like? Pick up a 'Discovery Backpack' or a 'Museum Toolkit' from the front desk to help with the littl'uns' explorations and learnings. (p60)

Maritime Museum of Tasmania Shipwrecks, whaling, yachts, rusty anchors – if there's anything uninteresting at this museum, let us know. (p70)

Mawson's Huts Replica Museum *Brrr,* Antarctica! Give the little blighters a concept of true hardship and see if their behaviour improves. (p70)

Top Tips

o Pick up the free *LetsGoKids* magazine (www.letsgokids.com.au) at the Hobart Visitor Information Centre for activity ideas.

o Kids under five travel free on Metro Tasmania public buses; over-fives receive discounted fares.

LGBTIQ+

Tasmania hasn't always been a safe place for the LGBTIQ+ community. The state decriminalised homosexuality in 1997 – and then only after a High Court challenge to the state's laws, triggered by a United Nations Human Rights Committee ruling. But these days it's a different story. Tasmania – and especially Hobart – are most definitely 'rainbow' in outlook.

OLGA KASHUBIN/SHUTTERSTOCK ©

Inclusive, Not Exclusive

It's a reflection of the city's population, rather than its attitudes, that Hobart's only dedicated gay bar closed during the COVID-19 pandemic and has yet to be replaced or reopen elsewhere. In the absence of a dedicated venue, when you're out and about it's more about finding a place to eat or drink with an open and inclusive vibe – and there are plenty to choose from, many of which are gay-owned and/ or operated.

Best Cafes

Criterion Street Cafe This pioneering inner-city cafe (Hobart's best coffee?) has been gay-friendly since day one. (p41)

Retro Cafe The quintessential Salamanca Place cafe has been going strong since before Tasmania repealed its anti-homosexuality laws. (pictured; p72)

Jackman & McRoss Hobart's top cafe is classy, classy, classy. (p118)

Best Pubs & Bars

Grand Poobah This central dance club and live-music venue hosts dedicated lesbian and queer nights, plus touring drag and glam cabaret shows. (p52)

Republic Bar & Café Hobart's lynchpin live-music venue serves up great food and even better tunes to a free-thinking crew. (p101)

The Winston This raffish North Hobart craft-beer pub is openminded and affable, with room at the bar for truckers of all predilections. (p99)

Four Perfect Days

Day One

Get your head into history mode with an amble around **Battery Point** (pictured; p108). Don't miss the photogenic cottages around Arthur Circus and the Hampden Rd cafes – try **Jackman & McRoss** (p118).

After lunch, wander down Kelly's Steps to historic **Salamanca Place** (p56) and check out the shops and galleries in the **Salamanca Arts Centre** (p70). Then, have a coffee at **Tricycle Cafe & Bar** (p74) before delving into Hobart's Antarctic heritage at the **Mawson's Huts Replica Museum** (p70) over near Constitution Dock. For dinner, head to **Flippers** (p73) for a fish-and-chip supper.

Afterwards, grab a drink at the upmarket **Glass House** (p78) in the floating Brooke Street Pier.

Day Two

On day two, recuperate over a big brunch and multiple coffees at **Retro Cafe** (p72) on Salamanca Place (if it's a Saturday, **Salamanca Market** (p81) will be pumping).

Afterwards, ferry out to **MONA** (p102) for an after-noon in the museum's amazing subterranean galleries. Grab a drink at one of MONA's bars, then cab-it back to **North Hobart** (p86) for dinner at **Pancho Villa** (p97) or **Roaring Grill** (p98).

For a crafty brew after dinner, try bohemian **The Winston** (p99) or a glass of vino at **Willing Bros** (p100). See what's screening at the art-house **State Cinema** (pictured; p101) or trundle down to the **Republic Bar & Café** (p101) for some live tunes.

Day Three

DARYL ARIAWAN/SHUTTERSTOCK ©

Start the day with a drive up Pinnacle Rd to **kunanyi/Mt Wellington** (p136) At the summit, scan the horizon or mountain-bike down the slopes on the **Mt Wellington Descent** (p137). Grab lunch at **Ginger Brown** (p119) in South Hobart afterwards.

At the foot of kunanyi/Mt Wellington are the **Cascade Brewery** (pictured; p128) and the **Cascades Female Factory Historic Site** (p132). Tour the ruins of the Female Factory prison before visiting Hobart's legendary brewery nearby.

In the evening, settle in for some super Italian at **Don Camillo** (p123) in upmarket Sandy Bay. Post-pasta drinks await back on buzzy Salamanca Place: try **Jack Greene** (p78) or **Waterman's Hotel** (p79).

Day Four

DAVID STEELE/SHUTTERSTOCK ©

Take it downtown. Grab breakfast at hip **Pilgrim Coffee** (p48), then hit the shops: **Cool Wine** (p41) for some booze, **Tommy Gun Records** (p41) for some music, or the Sunday-morning **Farm Gate Market** (pictured; p47) for all things organic, local and edible.

Backstreet **Templo** (p48) is a hit for lunch, then meander down to the outstanding **Tasmanian Museum & Art Gallery** (p60) near the waterfront for a shot of culture.

Treat yourself to a top-flight South American dinner at **Frank** (p77), then wander over to the laid-back **Hobart Brewing Company** (p78) to bend an elbow with the locals.

Need to Know

For detailed information, see Survival Guide (p140)

Currency
Australian dollar ($)

Language
English

Visas
All visitors to Australia need a visa, except New Zealanders. Apply online at www.border.gov.au.

Money
The major banks all have branches and ATMs around Elizabeth St Mall. There are also ATMs around Salamanca Place.

Mobile Phones
European phones will work on Australia's network, others won't. Use global roaming or a local SIM.

Time
Australian Eastern Standard Time (AEST; GMT/UCT plus 10 hours)

Tipping
Tipping is common but not mandatory.

Your Daily Budget

Budget: Less than $150
Double hostel room: $80–100
Budget pizza or pasta meal: $15–20
Local bus ride: from $3.30

Midrange: $150–300
Double room in a motel or B&B: $130–250
Cafe brunch: $20–30
Short taxi ride: $25

Top End: More than $300
Double boutique hotel room: from $250
Classy three-course restaurant meal: $80
MONA admission including ferry: $83

Advance Planning

Three months before During summer, Easter or June's Dark MOFO festival, book beds and restaurants early.

One month before Book popular tours (Mt Wellington Descent, Cascade Brewery, boat trips) and MONA tickets.

One week before Check the weather forecast: Hobart can sweat in November then freeze in December.

Useful Websites

Lonely Planet (www.lonelyplanet.com/australia/tasmania/hobart) Destination information.

Hobart & Beyond (www.hobartandbeyond.com.au) Places to stay, things to do and where to eat and drink.

Tasmanian Travel & Information Centre (www.hobart travelcentre.com.au) Info and booking hub.

 Arriving in Hobart

✈ From Hobart Airport

Hobart's 'international' airport is at Cambridge, 19km east of the city. Many visitors to the city rent a car (there are many rental desks in the airport terminal). A taxi into the city will cost around $50 and take about 20 minutes. Pre-booked shuttle buses (adult/child $19/14) with Hobart Airporter (www.airporterhobart.com.au) meet every flight and deliver you to city hotels.

🛳 From Devonport Ferry Terminal

If you're arriving by ferry from Melbourne, the big red boat spits you out in Devonport on Tasmania's northwest coast. It's a 3¼-hour drive from here to Hobart.

Getting Around

🚗 Car & Motorcycle

The quickest way to get around. Competition keeps car-rental prices reasonable.

🚕 Taxi

Hop from venue to venue.

🚶 Walking

Explore the city centre, waterfront and Battery Point under your own steam.

🚲 Bicycle

Hobart is hilly but super-scenic from the seat of a bike.

🚌 Bus

Use Hobart's clean, reliable, affordable public transport if you must, but services can be infrequent, especially after dark and on weekends. See www.metrotas.com.au.

RAFAEL BEN-AR/GETTY IMAGES ©

Hobart Neighbourhoods

Northern Hobart (p84)
The northern suburbs are where Hobart's bohemian soul shines through: spend a night eating and drinking along Elizabeth St to catch the vibe. Unmissable MONA is here too.

Central Hobart (p38)
Hobart's commercial hub is peppered with cafes, some interesting speciality shops, a Sunday-morning food market and some distracting pubs.

North Hobart ⊙

Cascades Female Factory Historic Site ⊙

⊙ *Cascade Brewery*

Salamanca Place & the Waterfront (p54)

The heart of Hobart's effervescent waterfront precinct is historic Salamanca Place – a gorgeous row of honey-hued 1830s sandstone warehouses, now home to eateries, drinkeries and have-a-look-sees.

Tasmanian Museum & Art Gallery

Salamanca Place

Battery Point

Battery Point, Sandy Bay & South Hobart (p106)

From the old whalers' and sailors' cottages in Battery Point to affluent Sandy Bay and atmospheric South Hobart, these three inner-city suburbs shine a light on Hobart's history

Explore
Hobart

Constitution Dock DARREN TIERNEY/SHUTTERSTOCK ©

Explore ✪
Central Hobart

Hobart's CBD is a long way from the high-rise architectural hedonism of the mainland Australian capitals. But among the stunted skyscrapers, Hobartians get busy with excellent cafes, endearing pubs, interesting shops and most of Hobart's budget accommodation. There are some top restaurants here, too, turning their backs on the more obvious glamour of the waterfront.

The Short List

○ **Farm Gate Market (p47)** *Wandering through Hobart's city-centre market: organic and local produce, baked goods, wine, coffee and beer breathe life into the Sunday city streets.*

○ **Hobart Convict Penitentiary (p45)** *Exploring another of Tasmania's prized clutch of historic convict sites.*

○ **City shopping (p52)** *Splashing some cash in the central outdoor-gear, music and food-and-wine shops.*

○ **Theatre Royal (p43)** *Taking a tour or catching a show at Australia's oldest theatre.*

○ **City coffee shops (p48)** *Charging up on caffeine at one (or three) of Hobart's hip coffee spots.*

Getting There & Around

🏃 Central Hobart is relatively flat and parking is limited – get around on foot.

🚌 All bus routes lead to central Hobart: bus into the city then walk around once you're there.

🚕 If you're staying in Sandy Bay or somewhere further flung, grab a cab into the city.

Neighbourhood Map on p42

Elizabeth St Mall (p41) ALEX CIMBAL/SHUTTERSTOCK ©

Walking Tour 🥾

City Centre Shuffle

Downtown Hobart isn't what you'd call a buzzing metropolis. There are no canyons of commerce, skyscrapers or subterranean train networks here. Instead what you'll find is an endearing city centre offering up some excellent speciality shops and arcades, quality spots for a coffee and some curious corners where Hobart's history peeps through the modernity.

Walk Facts

Start Molle St; bus stop 6, Davey St

End Criterion St; bus stop 2, Elizabeth St

Length 1.5km; one hour

❶ What Lies Beneath

Hobart's original water source, the **Hobart Rivulet** wiggles right through the middle of the CBD. In most places the rivulet has been built over, but on Molle St at the western edge of the city centre you can get a good look at it.

❷ Centrepoint Arcade

A wiggly shopping arcade built over the top of the Hobart Rivulet, split-level Centrepoint Arcade came into being in the 1980s. The shops here are fab: enter off Victoria St and wander your way past boutiques, cafes, jewellers, a perfumery, deli, florist, bookshop, newsagent, travel store...

❸ Cat & Fiddle Arcade

Cross Murray St, still following the course of the Hobart Rivulet below, and explore Cat & Fiddle Arcade, a two-tier shopping enclave which opened in 1962. A classic Hobart kids' experience is to see the animated Cat & Fiddle Clock playing out its pantomime hourly from 8am to 11pm.

❹ Mall Life

At the eastern end of Cat & Fiddle Arcade is the **Elizabeth St Mall** – a classic piece of 1980s town-planning that saw one of Hobart's busiest streets closed off to traffic. Still, it remains a busy shopping hub. An historic stone bridge over the rivulet was exposed during recent building works here: the resultant hole-in-the-mall now affords a rare window onto the chuckling rivulet below.

❺ Fine Wine

One of Hobart's best speciality shops is **Cool Wine** (☏03-6231 4000; www.coolwine.com.au; Shop 8, MidCity Arcade; ⏰9.30am-6.30pm Mon-Sat), a neat little independent booze vendor in the MidCity Arcade. Duck inside and peruse its selection of Tasmanian wines, beers and spirits.

❻ Cool Tunes

Hobart is a musical kinda town, and the best record shop in the city is **Tommy Gun Records** (☏03-6234 2039; www.facebook.com/tommygunhobart; ⏰10am-5.30pm Mon-Fri, 11am-3pm Sat, 10am-2pm Sun) on Elizabeth St. Stop by and check out the racks of vinyl (new and second-hand), plus metal T-shirts and DJ tech.

❼ Coffee on Criterion

Short and sweet Criterion St, between Liverpool and Bathurst Sts, has evolved into a simmering coffee hub. **Criterion Street Café** (☏03-6234 5858; mains $8-18; ⏰7am-4pm Mon-Fri, 8am-3pm Sat & Sun) was the trailblazer here, with new hole-in-the-wall coffee nooks like **Ecru** (☏0448 738 014; www.ecrucoffee.com.au; items from $3; ⏰7am-3pm Mon-Fri, 8.30am-12.30pm Sun) and **Villino** (☏03-6231 0890; www.villino.com.au; items $5-12; ⏰8am-4.30pm Mon-Fri, 9am-3pm Sat) popping up more recently.

0 — 200 m
0 — 0.1 miles

Patrick St

26
5
Hobart Convict Penitentiary

Campbell St

Brooker Ave

Railway Roundabout

Brooker Ave

Tasman Hwy

Tassielink

Brisbane St

Elizabeth St

Melville St

Argyle St

Hobart Police Station

Liverpool St

Theatre Royal

Campbell St

Gasworks Cellar Door

1

4

Evans St

Macquarie St

23

33

Bathurst St

Royal Hobart Hospital

Collins St

16

Hope & Anchor

Dunn Pl

Davey St

Victoria Dock

Murray St

22 12
20
11 Criterion St
3 25
Allport Library & Museum of Fine Arts

Bank Arc

Elizabeth St Mall

Cat & Fiddle Arc

The Place

19
Town Hall

Hobart Historic Tours

10

Mawson Place

Constitution Dock

Kings Pier Marina

15
32
13
27
14
Murray St
Centrepoint Arc

30

Street Eats @ Franko

7

8
Franklin Square

Elizabeth St

Morrison St

Brooke St

Elizabeth St Pier

Brooke St Pier

Sullivans Cove

24
29
St David's Cathedral
Victoria St
18
21

Government Offices

Parks & Wildlife Service

Murray St

Parliament House

Parliament Square

Princes Wharf

Goulburn St

Harrington St

Hobart Airporter

28
Collins St

17

Hobart Real Tennis Club
2

Supreme Court

St David's Park

Commonwealth Law Courts

Castray Esp

Salamanca Pl

BATTERY POINT

Redline Coaches

31

5

Barrack St

Macquarie St

Davey St

Sandy Bay Rd

Montpelier Rd

Salamanca Square

Hobart Rivulet

Markree House Museum

6

Wilmot St

Hampden Rd

Barrack St

Molle St

9
Army Museum of Tasmania

For reviews see	
⊙ Sights	p43
✖ Eating	p47
🍺 Drinking	p50
★ Entertainment	p51
🛍 Shopping	p52

Sights

Theatre Royal
HISTORIC BUILDING

1 ◎ MAP P42, C2

Hobart's prestigious (and very precious) Theatre Royal has been host to bombastic thespians since 1837, and despite a major fire in 1984, it remains Australia's oldest continuously operating theatre. (📞03-6233 2299; www.theatreroyal.com.au; 29 Campbell St; 1hr tour adult/child $15/10; ⊗tours 11am Mon, Wed & Fri)

Hobart Real Tennis Club
HISTORIC BUILDING

2 ◎ MAP P42, B4

Dating from 1875, this is one of only three such tennis courts in the southern hemisphere (the others are in Melbourne and Ballarat). Real (or 'Royal') tennis is an archaic form of the highly strung game, played in a jaunty four-walled indoor court. Visitors can watch, take a lesson ($50) or hire the court ($40 per hour per two players). (Royal Tennis Club; 📞03-6231 1781; www.hobarttennis.com.au; 45 Davey St, Hobart; ⊗9am-6pm Mon-Fri)

Allport Library & Museum of Fine Arts
MUSEUM

3 ◎ MAP P42, A3

The State Library is home to this excellent collection of rare books on the Australia-Pacific region, as well as colonial paintings, antiques, photographs, manuscripts, decorative arts and furniture. Special exhibits get dusted off for display several times a year, and there are monthly talks and seminars. Marvellously nerdy and interesting. (📞03-6165 5584; www.linc.tas.gov.au/allport; 91 Murray St, Hobart; admission free; ⊗9.30am-5pm Mon-Fri, to 2pm Sat)

Gasworks Cellar Door
WINERY

4 ◎ MAP P42, D2

If you want Tasmania's far-flung wine regions distilled into one experience, duck into the Gasworks Cellar Door, which is effectively a museum of wine and wine regions, but with the pleasures of tastings thrown in. There's a room dedicated to each region, with 16 wines to taste, and all wines displayed are on sale. (📞03-6231 5946; www.gasworkscellardoor.com.au; 2 Macquarie St, Hobart; tastings from $2.50; ⊗noon-4pm Sun-Wed, 11am-5pm Thu-Sat)

Caught in a One-way Web
ⓘ

Central Hobart's one-way system can take a while to get used to – is it overly complex for such a compact city? Take the sting out of the experience by leaving the car at your nearby accommodation (astutely booked after reading this) – thus also beating Hobart's dogged parking-meter wardens at their fiendish game.

Hobart
History

Aboriginal Hobart

Hobart's original inhabitants lived here harmoniously for many thousands of years, maintaining a culture of hunting, fishing and gathering, moving with the seasons and nature's harvest. The semi-nomadic Mouheneenner and Muwinina bands of the Southeast Aboriginal tribe called the area Nibberloonne. Mt Wellington, towering behind Hobart, was a place of refuge for the Muwinina, who called it Kunanyi – a name only recently reassigned to the mountain by the city council.

Colonisation & Convicts

In 1803 the first European arrivals in Van Diemen's Land pitched their tents at Risdon Cove on the Derwent's eastern shore, which became the site of the first massacre of the Mouheneenner. The colony relocated a year later to the site of present-day Hobart, where water running off Mt Wellington was plentiful: today's Hobart Rivulet was the colony's lifeblood.

When Britain's jails overflowed with sinners in the 1820s, tens of thousands of convicts were chained into rotting hulks and shipped down to Hobart Town to serve their sentences in vile conditions. Female convicts were incarcerated at the Female Factory in South Hobart; the worst of the male convicts went to Port Arthur, southeast of the city.

Into the 20th Century

In the 1840s, Hobart's sailors, soldiers, whalers and rapscallions boozed and brawled shamelessly in countless harbourside pubs. It could be argued that the city has only ever partially sobered up – the day Hobart's waterfront is no longer the place to go for a beer will be a sad day indeed – but today's patrons are more likely to be white-collared than bad company at the bar.

With the abolition of convict transportation to Tasmania in 1853, Hobart became marginally more moral and the town came to rely on the apple and wool industries for its fiscal fortitude. In the 20th century Hobart stuttered through the Great Depression and both World Wars, relying on the production of paper, zinc and chocolate, and the deep-water Derwent River harbour to sustain it.

Hobart Convict Penitentiary

HISTORIC SITE

5 ◎ MAP P42, B1

The courtrooms, cells and gallows at 'the Tench' had a hellish reputation in the 1800s, and every convict in Tasmania passed through here. The barracks are all gone, but the red-brick chapel remains solidly intact. Visits are by tour only, and include a 40-minute film, *Pandemonium,* projected onto the walls of the chapel, where convicts sat for church – it held up to 1500 people and was built atop 36 solitary-confinement cells.

Night-time **ghost tours** (adult/child/family $30/20/75; ⊘8pm Thu-Sat) should be booked ahead. (📞03-6231 0911; www.nationaltrust.org.au/places/penitentiary; cnr Brisbane & Campbell Sts; tours adult/child/family $25/15/65; ⊘tours 10am, noon, 2pm, 5.30pm & 7pm Tue-Sun)

Markree House Museum

MUSEUM

6 ◎ MAP P42, B5

This backstreet house is a window into life in 1920s Hobart, built for the Baldwin family in 1926 in the 'arts and crafts' architectural style of the day (lots of red brick). The garden is a treat, too. Combined tickets with the nearby Narryna Heritage Museum (p117) cost adult/child $16/10. (📞03-6165 7001; www.tmag.tas.gov.au/markree; 145 Hampden Rd, Battery Point; adult/child $10/4; ⊘10.30am-4.30pm Sat Oct-Apr, tours 3pm Tue-Sun year-round)

St David's Cathedral (p46)

SLOVEGROVE/GETTY IMAGES ©

Historic Architecture

Locals take for granted the gorgeous crop of heritage stone buildings around central Hobart: take a look at the **Theatre Royal** (p43), the **Town Hall** (Map p42, C3; 03-6238 2765; www.hobartcity.com.au; 50 Elizabeth St, Hobart; admission free; 8.15am-5.15pm Mon-Fri), **St David's Cathedral** and the marvelously eccentric **Hobart Real Tennis Club** (p43) for starters.

St David's Cathedral CHURCH

7 ◉ MAP P42, B4

Hobart's city-centre cathedral (1823) looks a tad austere, but inside the mood is serene and architecturally uplifting. Duck inside and regain your composure for a minute. Services 8am, 10am and 5.30pm on Sunday (or check out the virtual tour online). (03-6234 4900; www.saintdavids.org.au; 23 Murray St, Hobart; 8.30am-5pm Mon-Fri, 9am-5pm Sat, 8am-7.30pm Sun)

Franklin Square SQUARE

8 ◉ MAP P42, C4

Encircling a statue of Sir John Franklin, Lieutenant-Governor of Van Diemen's Land (aka Tasmania) from 1837–43, Franklin Sq is one of central Hobart's main public spaces (along with the Elizabeth St Mall). Sit on the grass, munch some lunch, wait for a bus, push some giant chess pieces around, or turn up on Friday night during summer for the Street Eats @ Franko (p47) food market. (www.hobartcity.com.au; cnr Macquarie & Elizabeth Sts; 24hr)

Army Museum of Tasmania MUSEUM

9 ◉ MAP P42, B6

The Anglesea Barracks were built adjacent to Battery Point in 1814. Still used by the army, this is the oldest military establishment in Australia. Inside is a volunteer-staffed museum, which runs 45-minute guided tours of the buildings and grounds on Tuesday. (Anglesea Barracks; 03-6237 7160; www.armymuseumtasmania.org.au; off Davey St, Hobart; adult/child/family $5/1/10; 9am-1pm Tue-Sat, guided tours 11am Tue)

Hobart Historic Tours WALKING

10 ◉ MAP P42, C3

Informative, entertaining walking tours of Hobart and historic Battery Point. There's a 1½-hour Old Hobart Pub Tour (5pm Thursday to Saturday), which sluices through some waterfront watering holes, a 1½-hour Historic Walk and a three-hour Grand Hobart Walk (both 2pm Wednesday to Sunday). (03-6234 5550; 16-20 Davey St, Hobart www.hobarthistorictours.com.au; tours $33-50)

Eating

Farm Gate Market

MARKET

11 🔒 MAP P42, A3

Bathurst St turns organic at this weekly foodie favourite that brings in primary producers from across the state – expect fresh fruit and veg, raw honey, BBQ octopus, cut flowers and organic kimchi and yoghurt. A seat in the sun on the road with a Lady Hester sourdough doughnut is the place to be on a Sunday morning. (📞03-6234 5625; www.farmgatemarket. com.au; Bathurst St, btwn Elizabeth & Murray Sts; ⏰8.30am-1pm Sun)

Bury Me Standing

CAFE $

12 🍴 MAP P42, B3

Stepping into this brilliant little coffee-and-bagel joint, run by a chipper Minnesotan who ended up in Hobart accidentally, is like waking into an old-time curiosity shop – skeleton wallpaper one side, bright swatches of paisley wrapping paper on the other. Seats are few and bagels are pot-boiled in the traditional method – don't go past the meat-free bagel dogs. (📞0424 365 027; www. facebook.com/burymestanding hobarttown; 83-85 Bathurst St; bagels $5-13; ⏰6am-4pm Mon-Fri, 7am-2pm Sat & Sun)

R Takagi Sushi

SUSHI $

13 🍴 MAP P42, B3

Central Hobart's best sushi spot – a favourite with desk jockeys – makes the most of Tasmania's great seafood. Udon noodles and miso also make an appearance. Gorgeous packaging to boot. (📞03-6234 8524; 132 Liverpool St, Hobart; sushi from $4; ⏰10.30am-5.30pm Mon-Fri, to 4pm Sat, 11.30am-3pm Sun)

Yellow Bernard

CAFE $

14 🍴 MAP P42, B3

With a global selection of interesting blends, Yellow Bernard (great name!) takes its coffee *very* seriously. If you're in a hippie mood, its chai – made with local honey and the cafe's own spice blend – is a perfect way to tune in while wandering Hobart's CBD. Biscuits and corners of cake to

Friday Night Street Food 🍽️

New to the Hobart foodie scene, **Street Eats @ Franko** (Map p42, C4; 📞03-6234 5625, 0408 543 179, www. streeteatsfranko.com.au; Franklin Sq, 70 Macquarie St; ⏰4.30-9pm Fri Nov-Apr) is a buzzy night market showcasing fabulous southern Tasmanian food, with live music and plenty to drink, too. Run by the same (rather busy) folks who organise the Sunday morning Farm Gate Market (p47).

City Vibes

During the day, downtown Hobart is a thriving hive of city workers, shoppers and cafe-goers – the Elizabeth St Mall, Cat & Fiddle Arcade and Centrepoint Arcade are commercially rampant – while multicultural eateries, cafes and little hole-in-the-wall coffee shops keep the office crew fed and fuelled. If you're after some hiking gear, the outdoor shops along Elizabeth St are where it's at. The city centre is also Hobart's public transport hub, with most buses leaving from the lower end of Elizabeth St or adjacent Franklin Sq.

Then, when the sun sets and the workers turn off computers and put on their coats, a kind of social vacuum cleaner sweeps the city streets, sucking up humans and reassigning them to the waterfront. It's true that you won't find a whole lot going on here after dark, but the shops, eateries and Sunday-morning Farm Gate Market are enough to keep you engaged for a few days.

take away. (☑03-6231 5207; www.yellowbernard.com; 109 Collins St, Hobart; items from $3; ⏲7am-4pm Mon-Fri)

Templo   ITALIAN $$

15 ⊗ MAP P42, A3

Unpretentious little Templo, on a nondescript reach of Patrick St, is a Hobart dining treasure. With only 20 seats (bookings essential), most of them around a communal table, and only three or four Italian-inspired mains to choose from, it's an exercise in selectivity and sharing (your personal space, and your food). Survey the pricey-but-memorable wine list at the cute bar. (☑03-6234 7659; www.templo.com.au; 98 Patrick St; plates $14-32; ⏲6pm-late Thu & Fri, noon-2.30pm & 6pm-late Sat-Mon)

Pilgrim Coffee   CAFE $$

16 ⊗ MAP P42, C3

With exposed bricks, timber beams and distressed walls, L-shaped Pilgrim is Hobart's hippest cafe. Expect wraps, panini and interesting mains (try the house black beans with pulled pork) and expertly prepared coffee. Fall into conversation with the locals at big shared tables. (☑03-6234 1999; www.facebook.com/Pilgrim.Coffee; 48 Argyle St, Hobart; mains $15-20; ⏲6.30am-4.30pm Mon-Fri, 8am-2pm Sat & Sun)

Mr Goodguy   ASIAN $$

17 ⊗ MAP P42, B5

Aiming for a future-Asian *Bladerunner* look, Mr Goodguy is a hawker-style restaurant revolving around a central bar, on the ground floor of the new ibis

Styles Hobart Hotel. Order the wallaby shank massaman curry, a plate of crispy-skin pork belly and a cold longneck of Tsingtao and work on your Ryan Gosling scowl. (☏03-6289 8516; www.mrgoodguy.com.au; 173 Macquarie St, Hobart; small plates $12-14, mains $20-28; ⏱6.30am-10pm)

Fico   ITALIAN $$

18 ✖ MAP P42, B4

This stylish Italian restaurant on Macquarie St somehow manages to feel intimate despite the traffic thundering past (jazz, bentwood chairs and moody lighting all help). Risottos and handmade pastas are the standouts – order the fresh spaghetti with sea urchin and a bottle of peppy Sicilian red. Sunday lunch is a set-menu affair ($75 per person). (☏03-6245 3391; www.ficofico.net; 151a Macquarie St, Hobart; mains $28-30, set menus $50-75; ⏱noon-3pm Fri-Sun, 6-10pm Tue-Sat)

Franklin   MODERN AUSTRALIAN $$$

19 ✖ MAP P42, C3

Regularly on lists of Australia's top restaurants, Franklin fills a lofty industrial space (the former *Hobart Mercury* newspaper printing room) and is all concrete, steel beams, cowhide and curtains. Everything is on show in the central kitchen, as the likes of wood-roasted octopus and Littlewood Farm lamb slip in and out of the 10-tonne oven. (☏03-6234 3375; www.franklinhobart.com.au; 30 Argyle St; shared plates $16-40; ⏱5pm-late Tue-Sat)

Shamrock Hotel (p51)

STEPHEN DWYER/ALAMY STOCK PHOTO ©

Urban Greek

GREEK $$$

20 ✖ MAP P42, A3

Fancy Mediterranean offerings in a former garage fitted out with bent copper lighting conduits, a timber bar, polished concrete floors and an intimidating Minotaur etched into the copperplate wall. Expect generous Greek classics done to perfection (moussaka, saganaki, charcoalgrilled octopus), family-style hospitality and imported Greek beers and wines. (📞03-6109 4712; www.urbangreekhobart.com; 103 Murray St; mains $30-49; ⏰5-10pm Mon-Thu & Sat, noon-2.30pm & 5-10pm Fri & Sun)

Astor Grill

STEAK $$$

21 ✖ MAP P42, B4

Indulge in old-school meaty treats at this sumptuous stalwart, in a blood-coloured 1920s artdeco brick building on the CBD fringe. Start with some oysters, then choose your prime cut, or perhaps the wallaby fillets with onion mash, beetroot and pepperberry sauce. Classy. (📞03-6234 3122; www.astorgrill.com.au; 157 Macquarie St, Hobart; mains $29-69; ⏰noon-4pm & 5.30-11.45pm Mon-Fri, 5.30-11.45pm Sat)

Drinking

New Sydney Hotel

PUB

22 🍺 MAP P42, A3

This low-key city pub is the best boozer in the CBD, with open fires, creative pub food (such as trout Kiev, or hazelnut and beetroot gnocchi; mains $15 to $38) and more than a dozen island craft beers and ciders on tap. No poker machines or TVs! (📞03-6234 4516; www.newsydneyhotel.com.au; 87 Bathurst St; ⏰noon-10pm Mon, to midnight Tue-Sat, 4-9pm Sun)

Coffee in the City

In this little southern city in a decade not so long ago, caffeine was something that came in instant granules, in a Coke can, or (if you were feeling particularly sophisticated) in a pallid cappuccino at a quasi-Mediterranean takeaway joint. But today, Hobart has truly woken up to real coffee, with a slew of new hole-in-the-wall bean bars opening up in the central city in recent years, and existing cafes lifting their espresso game to keep pace with the city's more discerning coffee palate. Late-night coffee shops have yet to take hold (aspiring Beat writers and Dylan-esque songwriters might have to convene at the pub instead) – but if you've just woken up and need a kick-starter, central Hobart's cafes have got you covered.

Rude Boy
BAR

23 MAP P42, A2

Old-time Havana mural, pastel-coloured stools, palm fronds painted on the windows, gallons of rum behind the bar – Rude Boy brings a little bit of the Caribbean into central Hobart. The cocktails here are killer: make have one 'Death in the Afternoon' (absinthe, lemon, passionfruit and sparkling wine) and you'll be inclined to stay for another. Reggae rules. (03-6236 9816; www.rudeboyhobart.com.au; 130 Elizabeth St, Hobart; 4pm-late Tue & Wed, 3pm-late Fri & Sat)

Shamrock Hotel
PUB

24 MAP P42, A4

No, it's not an Irish pub. The Shamrock is an old art-deco city pub, which has remained resolutely old-fashioned in its food, beer selection, vibe and decor while newer, hipper watering holes have tempted the punters away. Which means it's a great spot for a cold Cascade and a steak! Open fires and a couple of snug booths, too. (03-6234 3892; www.bestrestaurants.com.au; 195 Liverpool St, Hobart; 11am-10pm Mon-Sat, to 9pm Sun)

Entertainment

Playhouse Theatre
THEATRE

25 MAP P42, A3

This vintage city theatre (1864 – a former church) is home to the Hobart Repertory Theatre Society

Australia's Oldest Pub?

Depending on who you believe (don't listen to the barman at the Fortune of War in Sydney), the **Hope & Anchor** (Map p42, C3; 03-6236 9982; www.facebook.com/hopeandanchortav; 65 Macquarie St; 11.30am-late) in downtown Hobart is the oldest continually licensed pub in Australia (1807). The woody interior is festooned with nautical knick-knacks (duck up the stairs to see the museum-like dining room).

(musicals, Shakespeare, kids' plays). Book online. (03-6234 1536; www.playhouse.org.au; 106 Bathurst St, Hobart; box office opens 1hr prior to performances)

Brisbane Hotel
LIVE MUSIC

26 MAP P42, B1

The bad old Brisbane has dragged itself up from the pit of old-man, sticky-carpet alcoholism to be reinvented as a progressive, student-filled live-music venue. This is where anyone doing anything original, offbeat or uncommercial gets a gig: punk, metal, hip-hop and singer-songwriters. (03-6234 4920; www.facebook.com/thebrisbanehotelhobart; 3 Brisbane St, Hobart; 5-8.30pm Tue, noon-1am Wed & Thu, noon-4am Fri, 4pm-4am Sat, 4-10pm Sun)

Grand Poobah
LIVE MUSIC

27  MAP P42, B4

This bohemian city bar doubles as a music venue with everything from live bands to DJs, dance, cabaret and comedy. (📞0448 056 163; www.thegrandpoobahbar.com.au; 142 Liverpool St, Hobart; 🕙9pm-late Thu-Sat)

Village Cinemas
CINEMA

28 MAP P42, A4

An inner-city multiplex screening mainstream releases. Popcorn and sugary fizz galore. (📞1300 555 400; www.villagecinemas.com.au; 181 Collins St, Hobart; 🕙10am-late)

Shopping

Fullers Bookshop
BOOKS

29 MAP P42, B4

Hobart's best bookshop has a great range of literature and travel guides, plus regular book launches, signings and readings, and the writerly **Afterword Café** in the corner.

Fullers has been a true hub of the Hobart literary scene for almost a century. (📞03-6234 3800; www.fullersbookshop.com.au; 131 Collins St; 🕙8.30am-6pm Mon-Fri, 9am-5pm Sat, 10am-4pm Sun)

Playhouse Theatre (p51)

STEPHEN DWYER/ALAMY STOCK PHOTO ©

Hotel Horizons

Central Hobart's rather squat, inelegant collation of multistorey buildings looks set to be dwarfed by a new breed of southern skyscrapers, with several major new hotels sitting in the city council's inbox awaiting approval. Singaporean consortium Fragrance Group is behind three new hotel proposals here, including one already being built on Macquarie St, a proposed 120m-high tower on Davey St, and a 75m tower on Collins St. Whoa! Great for the economy and for fixing the city's notorious dearth of beds in the summer season, sure, but opponents are yelling out words like 'overkill', 'glut' and 'what happens in winter?'. Smaller hotel owners, too, are fearing a resultant price-cutting war that will drive them out of business. As always with divisive Tasmanian issues, the situation is a balancing act between vision and preservation, the now and the future, the local and the international. What will Hobart's downtown skyline look like in 10 years?

Cracked & Spineless   BOOKS

30 MAP P42, C3

We love a good secondhand bookshop (and don't care if the spines are cracked, absent or otherwise). This one is hidden up some steps at the back of a nondescript arcade, with $1 reads by the door and the odd new title in among the shambolic piles and aisles. (03-6223 1003; www.facebook.com/crackednspineless; 9/138 Collins St, Hobart; 9am-5.30pm Mon-Fri, to 4pm Sat)

Tasmanian Wine Centre   WINE

31 MAP P42, A5

Stocks a hefty range of local wines and can organise shipping and tastings for groups. The boss says the future of Tasmanian wine is sparkling whites... (03-6234 9995; www.tasmanianwinecentre.com.au; 201 Collins St, Hobart; 8am-6pm Mon-Fri)

Antiques to Retro   ANTIQUES

32 MAP P42, A3

Interesting furniture, vinyl, books, clothes, glassware and jewellery, old and not-so-old. The kitsch mid-century stuff is particularly cool. (03-6236 9422; www.antiquesto retro.com.au; 128 Bathurst St, Hobart; 11am-5pm Mon-Fri, 10am-4pm Sat)

Tasmanian Map Centre   MAPS

33 MAP P42, A2

Bushwalking maps, phrase books, fancy globes and Lonely Planet travel guides aplenty. (03-6231 9043; www.map-centre.com.au; 110 Elizabeth St, Hobart; 9.30am-5pm Mon-Fri, to 1.30pm Sat)

Explore

Explore

Salamanca Place & the Waterfront

Ground zero for most Hobart visitors, the waterfront is a broad concrete apron skirting Sullivans Cove, dotted with excellent restaurants, museums and accommodation. The vibe is bright, breezy and buzzy. Nearby is Salamanca Place, a well-preserved row of old sandstone warehouses hosting galleries, cafes, restaurants, pubs and bars. Salamanca Market erupts here every Saturday morning.

The Short List

○ **Salamanca Market (p81)** *Losing yourself among the stalls at this quintessential Hobart market.*

○ **Tasmanian Museum & Art Gallery (p60)** *Spending an afternoon learning about Hobart's history, and checking out colonial art.*

○ **Mawson's Huts Replica Museum (p70)** *Experiencing life in Antarctica as it was for Douglas Mawson and his crew in 1911.*

○ **Seafood (p73)** *Eating your way into some fresh fish and chips or a classy seafood dinner.*

○ **Waterfront drinking (p78)** *Winding down the day with a few drinks at Hobart's atmospheric waterside venues.*

Getting There

✈ Parking here is a drag; ditch the wheels and walk.

🚌 Bus services into Salamanca Place and the waterfront areas are affordable.

🚗 Cab-it in from North Hobart or Sandy Bay.

Neighbourhood Map on p68

Sullivan's Cove (p64) TARAS VYSHNYA/SHUTTERSTOCK ©

Top Experience 📷

Wander Through Salamanca Place

Dating back to Hobart's whaling and sailing heyday of the 1830s, Salamanca Place is a photogenic, 500m-long row of three- and four-storey sandstone warehouses. Gone are the sailors, whalers and wares: the buildings now host a fantastic collection of restaurants, cafes, bars, galleries, shops, pubs and performance spaces. The famed Salamanca Market consumes the entire street every Saturday morning.

◎ MAP P68, C7

Eating & Drinking

Interesting fact for the day: Salamanca Place takes its name from the Spanish province of Salamanca, where the Duke of Wellington claimed victory in the Battle of Salamanca in 1812. Something to discuss over a meal or an evening drink, perhaps – eating and drinking being the prime reasons you're here! So popular is the Salamanca scene that the Hobart City Council recently widened the footpath in front of the warehouses, to allow restaurants and bars more space for street-side tables and chairs. Wander along and see what kindles your appetite.

Salamanca Market

What started out as a couple of hippies selling raspberries in 1972 has evolved into a kilometre-long frenzy of food and commerce that consumes all of Salamanca Place every Saturday morning. With thousands of people here every week, Salamanca Market (p81) is something to behold: give yourself at least a few hours to wander its length and back again, a slow-shuffling circuit down one side of the stalls then back down the other. The cafes overflow, the buskers are in fine voice and (even when it's cold and wet) the atmosphere is downright convivial.

Salamanca Square

The big flat space out the back of Salamanca Place was once a quarry and then a car park. Then, in the mid-1990s, Salamanca Sq emerged. An adjunct, traffic-free space to the main thoroughfare, it's host to some great cafes and bars; the Hobart Book Shop (p83), one of the city's best; and Kathmandu (p83), the runaway-success outdoor company founded by resident Tasmanian Jan Cameron. There's also a kid-magnet fountain here and a few sunny patches of lawn to loll around on.

★ Top Tips

o Parking here can be a drag, even in the quietest of seasons (don't even think about it during the Saturday morning Salamanca Market (p81)); walk instead.

o For the pick of the fresh produce and antique knick-knacks, arrive at Salamanca Market early (8am should do it).

o Plan on spending at least a full day here: you'll need that long to digest your breakfast, lunch, afternoon tea, dinner...

✕ Take a Break

The list of Salamanca Place eating options might be long, but keep Retro Cafe (p72) at the top for coffee or brunch.

Jack Greene (p78) is open from lunchtime till late for beery libations.

Shifting Shoreline

It's hard to imagine now, but the Salamanca Place warehouses were once a lot closer to the water than they are today. No, the warehouses haven't moved, but the shoreline has: the broad concrete apron now skirting the whole of Sullivans Cove is largely built over reclaimed land. Merchants were once able to sail their ships right up to the front of the warehouses to offload/load their goods with ease (imagine how annoyed they'd be today!).

Salamanca Arts Centre

As with many of Tasmania's architectural relics, the Salamanca Place warehouses only survived the 20th century because no-one here had the money to knock them down. Thank goodness! Indeed, these chunky stone walls would take some shifting: step into the Salamanca Arts Centre (p70) for a close-up look...oh, and to check out the dozens of artists' studios, retail spaces, performance venues, cafes and galleries that comprise this artsy co-op.

Running since 1975, the SAC has become a vital hub of Hobart's artistic life, maintaining a hectic program of launches, events and performances to bolster its heady retail trade. If you're here on a Friday night, don't miss 'Rektango' at the **Salamanca Arts Centre Courtyard** (🕿 03-6234 8414; www.salarts.org.au/rektango; Salamanca Arts Centre Courtyard, Salamanca Pl; ⏲ 5.30-7.30pm Fri) – a free evening performance by one of several regular folk/world-music bands. Locals roll in, have a drink, a dance and generally let their hair down.

Hungry? Grab a coffee or some lunch at Tricycle Cafe & Bar (p74) or a bang-up Greek meal at Mezethes (p75), both tenants in the SAC complex.

Top Experience 📷
Explore the Tasmanian Museum & Art Gallery

Incorporating Hobart's oldest building, the Commissariat Store (1808), this revamped museum features Aboriginal and colonial art and relics, and excellent history and wildlife displays. 'TMAG', as it's known to friends and associates, occupies a special place in Hobartians' minds and memories. Every school child in the city has seen these rooms and walked these halls at some stage.

◉ **MAP P68, C2**

TMAG

☏ 03-6165 7000

www.tmag.tas.gov.au

Dunn Pl

admission free

🕙 10am-4pm, closed Mon Apr-Dec

Museum Highlights

Some of the most interesting things to see at the museum actually are the museum – historic buildings that form part of this huge, whole-city-block complex include the **Bond Store** (1824), **Commissariat Complex** (1808 – Tasmania's oldest surviving public building) and the **Private Secretary's Cottage** (1813), a little colonial cottage completely encircled by the museum.

Inside, don't miss the **Thylacine Gallery** on Level 1, telling the sad tale of the now (probably) extinct Tasmanian Tiger; and the **ningina tunapri** Tasmanian Aboriginal gallery, also on Level 1, which shines a light on Tasmania's oldest culture and country.

Nature-lovers will get a kick out of the **Tasmania: Earth & Life** display on Level 1, which digs into the island's geology and kooky contingent of flora and fauna.

Tasmanian Art

The main art galleries here are on the top floor (Level 2), with three spaces exhibiting a permanent collection of colonial, mid- and late-20th-century art, plus decorative arts. The colonial collection is particularly engaging, entitled 'Dispossessions and Possessions', with treasured works by arty notables such as Benjamin Duterreau and John Glover. The 20th-century galleries take a look at the influence of modernism on Tasmanian art, and the funky arts-and-crafts revival that happened here in the 1960s and '70s.

Guided Tours

Running from Wednesday to Sunday, free guided tours explore different areas of this sprawling, multilevel complex. Tours depart the main entry at 1pm and 2pm from September to May, and at 1.30pm from June to August. The 1pm tour visits the Welcome Garden and historic Commissariat Complex and Bond Store; the 2pm tour takes you into the main permanent exhibition and gallery spaces on

★ Top Tips

o Download a visitor map and guide from www.tmag.tas.gov. au (click on 'What's On' then 'Plan Your Visit').

o Free guided tours are a TMAG introduction. No bookings – just turn up (tours at 1pm and 2pm from Wednesday to Sunday).

o The Museum Shop sells Hobart's best travel-sized gifts (skip the tourist-tat in the Elizabeth St Mall).

✕ Take a Break

The museum's **Courtyard Cafe** (☏03-6165 7002; www.facebook.com/ museumcourtyardcafe; Tasmanian Museum & Art Gallery, Dunn Pl, Hobart; mains $6-16; ⏰9am-4pm Tue-Fri, 10am-4pm Sat & Sun) is good for coffee and cake.

Across Macquarie St from the museum is Australia's oldest pub, the Hope & Anchor (p115).

TMAG & The Tasmanian Aboriginal Advisory Council

Meeting quarterly, the Tasmanian Aboriginal Advisory Council advises TMAG in its capacity to research, preserve and interpret the state's Aboriginal culture and history (an area in which many Tasmanian museums have traditionally been very poor). Until such time as the proposed (and rather controversial) Tasmanian Aboriginal cultural precinct at nearby Macquarie Point gets the go-ahead, TMAG remains Tasmania's best source of information on local Aboriginal culture, heritage and contemporary life.

Levels 1 and 2. The 1.30pm tour adopts a 'Winter Highlights' theme, relating some quirky TMAG tales.

Also on offer are free themed and exhibition-specific tours running at 11am daily, Wednesday to Sunday. It's a changing program – check with the visitor information desk to see what's scheduled.

Kids' Stuff

Fully committed to showing your kids a good time, the museum runs dedicated family days on the last Sunday of every month, with heaps of hands-on, creative, interpretive experiences cued-up to help the little tackers get a handle on history. Similarly rich and educative are TMAG's excellent school holiday programmes: download a schedule of what's happening from www.tmag.tas.gov.au/learning_and_discovery/families.

On any day, free Discovery Backpacks (ages seven to 12) and Museum Toolkits (ages four to seven) are available from the front desk, filled with interesting objects and activities to help kids experience different aspects of the museum: history, art, the Southern Ocean, Antarctica and natural science.

Walking Tour 🥾

On the Waterfront

Hobart and the Derwent River are inextricably linked: the river sustained Aboriginal Tasmanians for millenniums; the river brought the English here in 1803; the river was Hobart's link to the world as it grew from a far-flung convict outpost. Take a walk around the waterfront to catch the nautical vibes.

Start Salamanca Pl; bus stop 4, Sandy Bay Rd

End Hunter St; bus stop D2, Franklin Sq

Length 1.5km; one hour

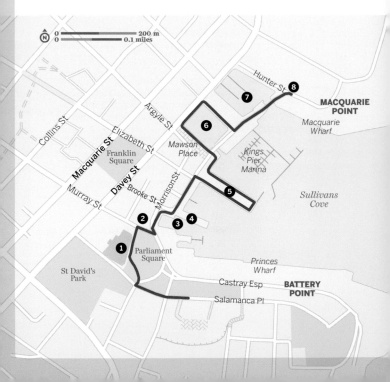

❶ Parliamentary Proceedings

From Salamanca Place, head across the lawns to gaze at the Parliament House (p67), which was originally built in 1840 as Hobart's customs house, keeping tabs on goods coming in and out of the port.

❷ Thirsty Work

Just across Murray St, the three-tiered, sandstone **Customs House Hotel** (📞03-6234 6645; www.customshotel.com; 1 Murray St, Hobart; ⏰7am-11pm Sun-Thu, to 12.30am Fri & Sat), which was licensed in 1846, is linked to Parliament House via a secret tunnel. It's a gritty, no-frills harbourside boozer – one of the last pubs on the waterfront to have resisted hipster-era trappings.

❸ Watermans Dock

Head for the water across Morrison St: Watermans Dock is the most modest of Hobart's docks, named for the watermen who ferried people around Hobart's shores in the mid-1800s. If the tide is low, traverse the concrete steps at the head of the dock.

❹ Brook St Pier

The flashy new floating Brook St Pier is where you catch the ferry to MONA (p102). It's a far cry from the old wooden ferry pier that became extremely busy when

Hobart's Tasman Bridge collapsed in 1975, and commuter ferries criss-crossed the river.

❺ Elizabeth St Pier

Most of the elegantly proportioned Elizabeth St Pier is consumed by an apartment hotel, eateries and bars. Walk out to the end and peer into the depths – Sullivans Cove is the world's second-deepest natural harbour (after Sydney).

❻ Constitution Dock

When the bedraggled boats in the Sydney to Hobart Yacht Race (p74) sail into town every New Year's Eve, Constitution Dock turns into party central. The rest of the year it's a rather soupy square of sea.

❼ Victoria Dock

If Constitution Dock is a party place, Victoria Dock is all about hard work. This is where Hobart's fleet of deep-sea fishing trawlers moors: count crayfish pots as you cross the swing bridge to Hunter St.

❽ Hunter St Warehouses

The Hunter St warehouses are eclectic, hosting restaurants, bars, the University of Tasmania School of Art and the outstanding **Henry Jones Art Hotel** (📞03-6210 7700; www.thehenryjones.com; 25 Hunter St; d $280-1200; 🅿✳@📶). Grab a glassful at the IXL Long Bar (p79) inside the Henry Jones.

Walking Tour 🥾

Hobart History Lesson

As Australia's second-oldest capital city, Hobart is riddled with interesting remnants of the 1800s. The waterfront, Battery Point and Salamanca Place are where you'll find most of them. Sandstone is everywhere, literally the building blocks of a colony, hacked out of cliff faces around the city and still looking photogenic, particularly in Hobart's honey-coloured evening light.

Start Macquarie St
Finish Salamanca Place
Length 3km; three hours

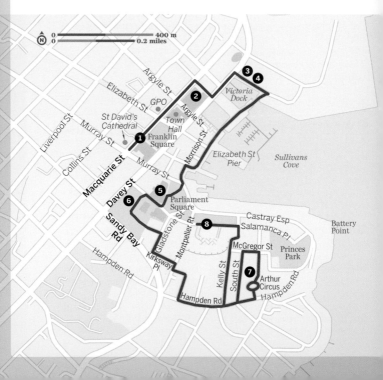

❶ Macquarie St

Hobart's grand boulevard, Macquarie St trucks past many of the city's classic old sandstone buildings, including St David's Cathedral (p46), dating from 1868, the 1906 **General Post Office** and the 1864 **Town Hall**, with a design based on Palazzo Farnese in Rome

❷ Tasmanian Museum & Art Gallery

Not only is TMAG (p60) a fabulous cache of historic Tasmania, the museum buildings themselves are also old. Check out the cavernous Bond Store (1824), the Private Secretary's Cottage (1813), and the Commissariat Complex (1808), Tasmania's oldest public building.

❸ Henry Jones Art Hotel

Built over a long-since-buried isthmus to Hunter Island, the Hunter St warehouses mirror those in Salamanca Place across Sullivans Cove. The outstanding Henry Jones Art Hotel (p65) is here, built inside the former IXL jam factory.

❹ Take a Break

As you wander over to the Henry Jones Art Hotel on Hunter St, duck into the in-house cafe **Jam Packed** (☏03-6231 3454; www.thehenryjones. com; Henry Jones Art Hotel, 27 Hunter St, Hobart; mains $9-20; ☉7.30am-3pm; ☏) for a rejuvenating coffee. is here, built inside the former IXL jam factory.

❺ Parliament House

Cross the swing bridge and fishtail across the waterfront, passing historic Victoria Dock, Constitution Dock and Watermans Dock. Tasmania's noble sandstone **Parliament House** (☏03-6212 2200; www.parliament.tas.gov.au/ parliament/tours.htm; admission free; ☉tours 9.30am & 2.30pm Mon-Fri on non-sitting days) is just across Murray St. Tours are available when parliament isn't in session.

❻ St David's Park

Resist the photogenic frontage of Salamanca Pl for now and turn right to detour through St David's Park, the site of Hobart's original cemetery, with a picturesque pergola and walls lined with relocated colonial gravestones.

❼ Battery Point

Cut through Salamanca Mews, jag right onto Gladstone St, left onto Kirksway Pl then right onto Montpellier Retreat, arcing uphill into Battery Point (p108), Hobart's oldest residential area. Duck into the Hampden Rd cafes and spin around the improbably quaint Arthur Circus.

❽ Salamanca Place

Bumble down Kelly's Steps (p113), an 1839 sandstone link between Battery Point and the redeveloped 1830s warehouses of Salamanca Place (p56), Hobart's food-and-drink epicentre. Enjoy!

Salamanca Place & the Waterfront

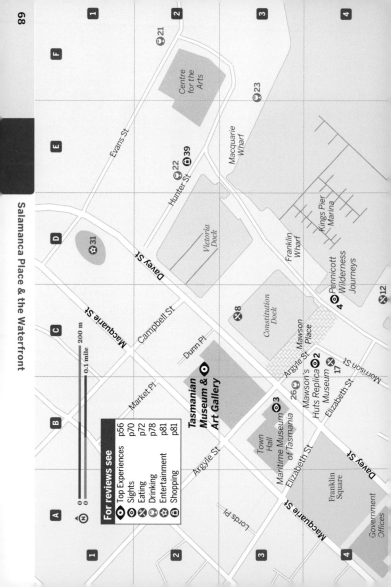

For reviews see
◉	Top Experiences	p56
◎	Sights	p70
✕	Eating	p72
✕	Drinking	p78
✿	Entertainment	p81
🛍	Shopping	p81

Centre for the Arts

Macquarie Wharf

Victoria Dock

Kings Pier Marina

Franklin Wharf

Pennicott Wilderness Journeys

Constitution Dock

Mawson's Huts Replica Museum

Maritime Museum of Tasmania

Town Hall

Tasmanian Museum & Art Gallery

Franklin Square

Government Offices

Evans St
Davey St
Campbell St
Hunter St
Macquarie St
Market Pl
Dunn Pl
Argyle St
Mawson Place
Morrison St
Elizabeth St
Davey St
Elizabeth St
Macquarie St
Lords Pl

200 m
0.1 mile

Sights

Salamanca Arts Centre

ARTS CENTRE

1 ◎ MAP P68, C7

The nonprofit Salamanca Arts Centre has been here since 1977 and occupies seven Salamanca warehouses. It's home to dozens of arts organisations and individuals, including excellent shops, galleries, theatres, studios, performing-arts venues, a cheese shop, a couple of cafes and public spaces.

Don't miss the free Friday evening Rektango (p59) hoedown in the Salamanca Arts Centre Courtyard out the back. (SAC; ☏03-6234 8414; www.salarts.org.au; 65-77 Salamanca Pl; ☺shops & galleries 9am-5pm)

Mawson's Huts Replica Museum

MUSEUM

2 ◎ MAP P68, C4

This excellent waterfront installation is a model of one of the huts in which Sir Douglas Mawson's Australasian Antarctic Expedition team, which set sail from Hobart, hunkered down from 1911 to 1914. The replica is painstakingly exact (Mawson's tiny keyboard, a sledge and an ice axe are actually originals) and a knowledgeable guide is on hand to answer your Antarctic enquiries. Imagine 18 men living here, dining on penguin stew...

Entry fees go towards the upkeep of the original huts at Cape Denison in Antarctica. (☏03-6231 1518, 1300 551 422; www.mawsons-huts-replica.org.au; cnr Morrison & Argyle Sts; adult/child/family $15/5/35; ☺9am-6pm Oct-Apr, 10am-5pm May-Sep)

Maritime Museum of Tasmania

MUSEUM

3 ◎ MAP P68, B3

Highlighting shipwrecks, boat building, whaling and Hobart's unbreakable bond with the sea, the Maritime Museum of Tasmania (out the back of the town hall) has an interesting (if a little static) collection of photos, paintings, models and relics (try to resist ringing the huge brass bell from the *Rhexenor*). Kids under 13 get in free. (☏03-6234 1427; www.maritimetas.org; 16 Argyle St; adult/child/family $10/8/20; ☺9am-5pm)

Pennicott Wilderness Journeys

BOATING

4 ◎ MAP P68, C4

Pennicott offers several outstanding boat trips around key southern Tasmanian sights, including trips along Bruny Island, the Tasman Peninsula and the Iron Pot Lighthouse south of Hobart. The 7½-hour Tasmanian Seafood Seduction trip, replete with a Neptune's bounty of abalone, lobster, oysters and salmon, is a winner for fans of all things fishy. (☏03-6234 4270; www.pennicottjourneys.com.au; Dock Head Bldg, Franklin Wharf; tours adult/child from $125/100; ☺7am-6.30pm)

Hobart Bike Hire

CYCLING

5 ⊙ MAP P68, B5

Just in from the Brooke Street Pier, this bike-hire shop has lots of ideas for self-guided tours around the city or along the Derwent River to MONA museum. Maps, locks and helmets are included; kids' trailers, tag-alongs, electric bikes and tandems are available, and you can keep the bike overnight (extra $10) if you're missing your dawn rides. (📞 0447 556 189; www. hobartbikehire.com.au; 1a Brooke St; bike/e-bike hire per day from $25/45; ⊙9am-5pm)

Gourmania

FOOD & DRINK

Fabulous, flavour-filled walking tours run by passionate local foodies, taking in Salamanca Pl and central Hobart. Expect plenty of tasting opportunities and chats with restaurant, cafe and shop owners. Saturday sees a two-hour Salamanca Market tour ($95). (📞 0419 180 113; www. gourmaniafoodtours.com.au; tours $129-139)

Drink Tasmania

DISTILLERY

Tasmanian whisky is riding a wave of awards and popularity, and a day tour with this passionate outfit visits three or four southern distilleries for tastings of top Tassie single malts. Minimum four people. Wine and beer tours also available. (📞 0475 000 120; www. drinktasmania.com.au; whisky tour per person from $299; ⊙Fri & Sun)

Pennicott Wilderness Journeys

Macquarie Point & MONA ⓘ

What an opportunity! The vast area of industrial port land known as Macquarie Point, adjacent to Hobart's waterfront, is ripe for redevelopment. In 2016, the founder of MONA, eccentric/genius David Walsh, announced plans to build a $2 billion cultural precinct here, acknowledging and celebrating 40,000 years of continuous Aboriginal history in the state. Visionary and long overdue in its intent towards reconciliation, certainly, but opponents claim ongoing port functions, including logging exports, are at odds with tourism and that the two could not co-exist. Hobart's Lord Mayor also weighed in, suggesting that such a project might be 'guilt-ridden' if not done tastefully (...perhaps she'd seen the infamous poop machine at MONA). Whatever happens, if David Walsh is involved, it's sure to be interesting – watch this space!

Red Decker BUS

Commentated sightseeing on an old London double-decker bus. Buy a 20-stop, hop-on-hop-off pass (valid for one or two days) or do the tour as a 90-minute loop. You can also add a Cascade Brewery tour ($65, including the bus loop) or minibus trip to the summit of kunanyi/Mt Wellington (adult/child $70/45) to the deal. (☏03-6236 9116; www.reddecker.com.au; 20-stop pass adult/child/family 24hr $35/20/90, 48hr $40/25/110)

Tours Tasmania TOURS

Small-group full-day trips from Hobart, including trips to Port Arthur, Hastings Caves and a 'Mt Field, Wildlife & Mt Wellington' tour with lots of walks and waterfalls (adult/concession $130/120). Park fees included; BYO lunch. (☏1800 777 103; www.tourstas.com.au)

Hobart Historic Cruises CRUISE

6 ◉ MAP P68, B6

Chug up or down the Derwent River from Hobart's waterfront on cute old ferries. Also runs longer lunch (adult/child/family $35/35/120) and dinner ($58/55/180) cruises travelling both up and down the river. Call for times and bookings. (☏03-6200 9074; www.hobarthistoriccruises.com.au; Murray St Pier, Hobart; 1hr cruises adult/child/family $25/22.50/70; ☺cruises 11am-4pm)

Eating

Retro Cafe CAFE $

7 ✕ MAP P68, B7

So popular it hurts, funky Retro is ground zero for Saturday brunch among the market stalls (or any day, really). Masterful breakfasts, bagels, salads and burgers interweave with laughing staff, chilled-out jazz and the whirr and bang of the coffee machine. A classic Hobart cafe. (☎03-6223 3073; 31 Salamanca Pl, Hobart; mains $11-20; ⏰7.30am-5pm Mon-Fri, 8am-5pm Sat & Sun; ✈)

Flippers

FISH & CHIPS $

8 ⓧ MAP P68, C3

There are four floating fish punts moored in Constitution Dock, selling fresh-caught seafood either uncooked or cooked. Our pick is Flippers, an enduring favourite with a voluptuous fish-shaped profile. Fillets of flathead and curls of calamari come straight from the deep blue sea and into the deep fryer. The local seagulls will adore you.

Grab dessert from the floating ice-cream punt next door. (☎03-6234 3101; www.flippersfishandchips. com.au; 1 Constitution Wharf; fish & chips $12-17; ⏰9am-9.30pm; ⛴)

Daci & Daci

BAKERY $

9 ⓧ MAP P68, A5

A 2018 refurb has this stylish bakery-cafe looking all leather and latte, and suitably slick for the steady flow of public servants and parliamentary folk. The seasonal soup with house bread is great value at $12.50, and the dessert list is extensive. Sit inside if it's wet, or on the split-level deck jutting out into Murray St if it's not. (☎03-6224 9237; www. dacianddacibakers.com.au; 11 Murray St; mains $10-18; ⏰7am-5pm)

Salamanca Place & the Waterfront Eating

Flippers

JAX1O289/SHUTTERSTOCK ©

Machine Laundry Café CAFE $

10 MAP P68, C8

Washing machines and dryers; pavement chessboard; retro styling; parmesan, caramelised onion and spinach pancakes; and the 'mental lentil' panini...breakfast or lunch is never dull at this brilliant and bright cafe squished into a corner of Salamanca Sq. (03-6224 9922; 12 Salamanca Sq; mains $11-23; 7.30am-5pm Mon-Sat, from 8am Sun)

Tricycle Cafe & Bar CAFE $

11 MAP P68, D8

This cosy red-painted nook inside the Salamanca Arts Centre (p70) serves up a range of cafe classics (BLTs, toasties, scrambled free-range eggs, salads, house-brewed chai and Fair Trade coffee), plus awesome daily specials (braised Wagyu rice bowl with jalapeño cream – wow!). Wines by the glass from the bar. (03-6223 7228; www.facebook. com/tricyclecafeandbarsalamanca; 77 Salamanca Pl, Hobart; mains $8-20; 8.30am-4pm Mon-Fri, to 3pm Sat)

Fish Frenzy SEAFOOD $$

12 MAP P68, C4

A casual, waterside fish nook, overflowing with fish fiends and brimming with fish and chips, fishy salads (warm octopus with yoghurt dressing) and fish burgers. The eponymous 'Fish Frenzy' ($21) delivers a little bit of everything. Quality can be inconsistent, but good staff and buzzy harbourside vibes compensate. No bookings. (03-6231 2134; www.fishfrenzy.com. au; Elizabeth St Pier, Hobart; mains $13-35; 11am-9pm;)

Kosaten Japanese Restaurant JAPANESE $$

13 MAP P68, E7

We could say this darkened Japanese bunker in an old stone ordnance store near Salamanca Place is a sushi-train joint, but

Sydney to Hobart Yacht Race

Arguably the world's greatest and most treacherous open-ocean yacht race, the **Sydney to Hobart Yacht Race** (www.rolexsydney hobart.com; Dec) winds up at Hobart's Constitution Dock some time around New Year's Eve. As the storm-battered maxis limp across the finish line, champagne corks pop and weary sailors turn the town upside down. On New Year's Day, find a sunny spot by the harbour, munch some lunch from the **Taste of Tasmania** (www. thetasteoftasmania.com.au; Princes Wharf; Dec-Jan) food festival and count spinnakers on the river. New Year's resolutions? What New Year's resolutions?

GREGORY J SMITH/SHUTTERSTOCK ©

Boats for the Sydney to Hobart Yacht Race

that would be underselling it. Plates of gorgeously prepared Wagyu, pork belly, soft-shell crab tempura and grilled scallops travel the train tracks along with more predictable sushi and sashimi, best consumed with a cold Asahi. Good vegetarian options, too. (☎03-6135 4018; www. kosaten.com.au; 17 Castray Esplanade, Battery Point; small plates $5-15; ⊙11am-3pm & 5pm-late Mon-Sat; ⏶)

Maldini ITALIAN $$

14 MAP P68, C7

A midrange Italian joint steadily climbing the culinary rungs, with essential pasta and risotto dishes offered alongside peppy mains such as chilli-marinated chicken breast and prosciutto-wrapped eye fillet. Tiramisu and grappa polish the palate and close out the night. Lovely interiors. (☎03-6223 4460; www.maldinirestaurant.com. au; 47 Salamanca Pl, Hobart; breakfast mains $9-25, lunch & dinner $27-43; ⊙8am-late)

Mezethes GREEK $$

15 MAP P68, C8

Tried and true Greek dishes and Adonis-like staff come together perfectly at Mezethes. All the classics (moussaka, souvlaki, lamb, fish, saganaki, baklava) plus, in true Hellenic style, a dazzling array of starters. The seafood platter ($38 per person) is hard to beat. Grab an outdoor table on a warm evening or a takeaway souvlaki (kebab) at lunch. (☎03-6224 4601; www.mezethes.com.au; 77 Salamanca Pl, off Woobys La, Hobart; mains breakfast $12-20, lunch & dinner $26-38; ⊙8.30am-late)

Hobart's
Antarctic Links

Tasmania was the last chunk of Gondwanaland to break free from Antarctica, which is now about 2500km south of Hobart. As the planet heats up and scientists forecast melting Antarctic ice, Hobart is becoming one of the world's leading Antarctic research and gateway cities.

Antarctic Research

The **Australian Antarctic Division** has its HQ in suburban Kingston south of Hobart, but there's also the CSIRO's **Division of Marine Research**, further along the waterfront from Salamanca Place; and the University of Tasmania's sleek **Institute of Antarctic and Southern Ocean Studies** building just across the road from Salamanca Place (also home to the **Antarctic Climate and Ecosystems Cooperative Research Centre**, tasked with understanding Antarctica's role in the global climate system and projecting climate change impacts).

The Antarctic Division's garish orange research vessel *Aurora Australis* and the CSIRO's boats *Southern Surveyor* and MV *Franklin* are regulars at the Hobart wharves. The *Aurora Australis*, in particular, has become a Hobart icon, much photographed and welcomed into port like a returning warrior.

Mawson's Huts

Next to Constitution Dock on the Hobart waterfront, the fascinating Mawson's Huts Replica Museum (p70) recreates the famed explorer Douglas Mawson's century-old Antarctic huts in intricate detail.

To much fanfare, Mawson and his crew of 18 set sail from Hobart in 1911, bound for the great southern continent, still largely unknown at the time (no-one had set foot on Antarctica prior to 1895). When Mawson arrived, he and his men built four timber huts at Cape Denison and established the first permanent Australian Antarctic base.

Mawson's huts are still standing, but, under constant assault by the weather, are in various states of disrepair: all profits from this museum go towards their preservation. Inside, the museum is brilliantly detailed and atmospheric: it's not hard to imagine 19 men living and working in these cramped confines, while outside the blizzards raged.

Aløft

MODERN AUSTRALIAN $$$

16 MAP P68, C5

Boldly claiming itself as Hobart's top restaurant, angular Aløft occupies a lofty eyrie atop the floating Brooke St Pier. Menu hits include silken tofu with burnt onion and baby leeks, and crispy duck leg with kimchi. If you can drag your gaze away from the view, service and presentation are both excellent, in an unpretentious Hobart kinda way.

The banquets are great value (including vegan and vegetarian options). (☎03-6223 1619; www.aloftrestaurant.com; Brooke St Pier; plates $14-36, banquets from $80; ⏰6pm-late Tue-Sat; ✈)

Frank

SOUTH AMERICAN $$$

17 MAP P68, C4

At the base of the much-maligned Marine Board Building, Frank brings fabulous South American–inspired flavours to the Hobart waterfront. Everything is designed for sharing, from empanadas to small plates (crispy squid, confit lamb ribs), vegetable dishes (charred sweet potato and goat's-milk curd), and sensational steaks (big ones cost up to $89). Frank is one well-dressed hombre, with super-hip interior design. (☎03-6231 5005; www.frankrestaurant.com.au; 1 Franklin Wharf, Hobart; mains $39-49; ⏰11am-10.30pm)

Aurora Australis

Old-School Pubs

There are so many new craft-beer joints, cocktail spots and cafe-bars around here it's hard to know where to start. For a more down-to-earth beer experience, follow perplexed-looking locals into an old-school waterside pub: try the Telegraph Hotel (p115) or Customs House Hotel (p65), both on Morrison St.

Blue Eye   SEAFOOD $$$

18 ⊗ MAP P68, D7

Ignore the slightly clinical decor and dive into some of Hobart's best seafood. Stand-outs include scallop linguine, curried seafood chowder with grilled sourdough, and a terrific seafood pie with parsley-and-spinach cream. Moo Brew pilsner on tap and a Tasmanian-skewed wine list complete a very zesty picture. Pricey, but top-quality all the way. (☑03-6223 5297; www.blueeye.net.au; 1 Castray Esplanade, Hobart; mains $30-50; ☉5-9pm Mon, 11am-9pm Tue-Sat)

Drinking

Jack Greene   BAR

19 🍸 MAP P68, C7

The gourmet burgers here nudge $20, but atmospheric Jack Greene (a European hunting lodge on the run?) is worthwhile if you're a wandering beer fan. Glowing racks of bottled brews fill the fridges, and there are at least 16 beers on tap from around Australia and New Zealand. Occasional acoustic troubadours perch next to the stairs. (☑03-6224 9655; www.jackgreene.com.au; 49 Salamanca Pl, Hobart; ☉11.30am-late)

Glass House   COCKTAIL BAR

20 🍸 MAP P68, C5

The very fancy Glass House sits in the prow of the floating Brooke St Pier, sandwiched between Aløft (p77) and Brooke St Larder, with a huge window-wall affording uninterrupted views across the Derwent River. Put on your best duds, order a martini with sheep-whey vodka and soak it all in. Fab bar food too (small plates $12 to $36). (☑03-6223 1032; www.theglass.house; Brooke St Pier; ☉noon-late)

Hobart Brewing Company   CRAFT BEER

21 🍸 MAP P68, F2

In a big red shed on Macquarie Point, fronted by the Red Square community space (fancy a haircut from a caravan hair salon?), Hobart Brewing Company is doing good things with craft beer. There are up to a dozen creative brews on tap, plus regular live music and the **Hobart Blues, Brews and Barbecues** festival around February or March. (☑03-6231 9779; www.hobartbrewingco.com.au; 16 Evans St; ☉3-10pm Wed & Thu, to 11pm Fri, 2-11pm Sat, 2-5.30pm Sun)

IXL Long Bar

BAR

22 🍸 MAP P68, E2

Prop yourself at the glowing bar at the Henry Jones Art Hotel (p65) and check out Hobart's fashionistas over a honey porter. If there are no spare stools at the bar, flop on to the leather couches in the hotel lobby. Moo Brew on tap, killer whiskies and live jazz Thursday to Saturday. (☏03-6210 7700; www.thehenryjones.com; Henry Jones Art Hotel, 25 Hunter St, Hobart; ⏰5-10.30pm Mon-Thu, 3-10.30pm Fri & Sat, 5-9pm Sun)

Evolve

LOUNGE

23 🍸 MAP P68, F3

What's prehistorically old is new at this sophisticated spirits bar inside the MACq 01 hotel, where you'll drink among an array of fossils, including a mammoth tusk and a Russian cave bear. Some of the whiskies – including the 1950 Glen Grant single malt (got a spare $7000?) – are almost museum pieces themselves. (☏03-6210 7656; http://evolvespiritsbar.com.au; MACq 01, 18 Hunter St; ⏰5pm-1am)

T-42°

BAR

24 🍸 MAP P68, D5

Stylish waterfront T-42° makes a big splash with its food (mains $18 to $32), but also draws well-dressed, late-week barflies with its minimalist interior, spinnaker-shaped bar and ambient tunes. If you stay out late enough on Friday or Saturday night, breakfast offers redemption from your nocturnal misdemeanours. (☏03-6224 7742; www.tav42.com.au; Elizabeth St Pier, Hobart; ⏰10am-10pm Mon-Thu, 10am-1.30am Fri, 8.30am-1.30am Sat, 8.30am-10pm Sun)

Waterman's Hotel

CRAFT BEER

25 🍸 MAP P68, B7

'Since 1840' is the tag-line here... Well, the building maybe. But 'WBM' is one of a new brigade of Salamanca Place booze rooms, focused on excellent craft and small-batch beers and live music Thursday to Saturday. Order a pint of Iron Pot Rye Porter from Hobart Brewing Company (p78) and head for the moody row of booths. 'Lawn' courtyard out the back. (WBM; ☏0424 176 745; www.watermanshotel.com.au; 27 Salamanca Pl, Hobart; ⏰11am-2am Tue-Sat, to midnight Sun)

Lark Distillery

DISTILLERY

26 🍸 MAP P68, B3

The pioneer and patriarch of Tasmanian distilleries, Lark has a moody, low-slung cellar door and whisky bar at the water's edge (the actual distillery is in the Coal River Valley, 20 minutes' drive away). Work your way along the whisky wall, and if the weather's right, sit out the back in the whisky garden overlooking Constitution Dock.

Distillery tours ($80), which include tastings from the cask, start at the cellar door before heading out to the good stuff. Tours run at 10.30am and 1.30pm daily

Life by the Harbour

These waterside precincts embody Hobart at its most hyperactive. Well, maybe just active. Either way, the visual appeal of the Salamanca Place sandstone warehouses and shimmering Sullivans Cove with its waterfront bars, pubs, restaurants and resident fishing fleet is undeniable (bring your camera). There are enough places to eat and drink here to keep you busy for months, but give yourself a few days to soak it all up – perhaps starting at the Salamanca Place side of the cove, working your way around the waterfront and back again. Even if you leave the area to shop, check out museums, visit MONA etc, you'll probably find yourself drawn back here at night when the pubs and bars really get rockin'.

except Thursday. (📞03-6231 9088; www.larkdistillery.com; 14 Davey St; ⏲noon-8pm Sun-Thu, to 11pm Fri & Sat)

Grape   WINE BAR

27 🚇 MAP P68, C7

In search of civility amid the nocturnal Salamanca fray? Grape is possibly your best bet, a woody wine bar with a superb list of Tasmanian drops, wandering occasionally across Bass Strait (like most Tasmanians) into Victoria and South Australia. Beers are mainstream; cocktails are more interesting. Love the cork-filled bar frontage. (📞03-6224 0611; www.grapebar.com.au; 55 Salamanca Pl, Hobart; ⏲11am-11.30pm Sun-Thu, to 2am Fri & Sat; 🛜)

The Whaler   PUB

28 🚇 MAP P68, B7

Until several years ago this pub was called 'Knopwoods Retreat', an endearing old boozer and a

perennial Friday-night favourite. The Whaler is doing its best to live up to the tradition, its unpretentious service and interiors making it something of an incongruity on the otherwise highly polished Salamanca Place. (📞03-6200 1854; www.thewhaler. com.au; 39 Salamanca Pl, Hobart; ⏲11am-late)

Salamanca Whisky Bar   BAR

29 🚇 MAP P68, C8

The decor here is magical – leather, brass, cowhide, well-worn floorboards and sandstone, illuminated only by candles – and the vibe is conversational. Perhaps you'd like to discuss the prices, which are lofty to say the least. For now, we're prepared to be forgiving because their Blood & Sand cocktail is awesome (whisky, sweet vermouth, blood orange and cherry). (📞0488 000 070; 3/63 Woobys La, Hobart; ⏲10am-midnight Mon-Fri, 8am-midnight Sat & Sun)

Entertainment

Peacock Theatre
THEATRE

30 ⭐ MAP P68, C8

This intimate theatre (around 150 seats) is inside the artful Salamanca Arts Centre (p70), along with a handful of other small performance spaces. Hosts theatre, dance, music and film. (📞03-6234 8414; www.salarts.org.au/venue/peacock-theatre; Salamanca Arts Centre, 65-77 Salamanca Pl, Hobart; ⏲box office 9am-5pm)

Federation Concert Hall
CLASSICAL MUSIC

31 ⭐ MAP P68, D1

Welded to the Hotel Grand Chancellor, this concert hall resembles a huge aluminium can leaking insulation from gaps in the panelling. Inside, the Tasmanian Symphony Orchestra does what it does best. (📞1800 001 190, 03-6232 4450; www.tso.com.au; 1 Davey St; ⏲box office 10am-4pm Mon-Fri)

Irish Murphy's
LIVE MUSIC

32 ⭐ MAP P68, B7

Pretty much what you'd expect from any out-of-the-box Irish pub: crowded, lively, affable and dripping with Guinness. Free live music of varying repute from Tuesday to Sunday nights (open-mic on Tuesday; originals on Wednesday). (📞03-6223 1119; www.irishmurphys.com.au; 21 Salamanca Pl, Hobart; ⏲11am-midnight Sun-Tue, to 1am Wed & Thu, to 3am Fri, 10am-3am Sat)

7D Cinema
CINEMA

33 ⭐ MAP P68, B8

Something new for Hobart: quick-fire, short 3D film 'rides' where you sit on a moving simulator. No scheduled ticketing – just turn up and jump on the next ride. (📞03-6224 6825; www.7dcinema.com.au; 8 Montpelier Retreat, Hobart; adult/child $15/13; ⏲10am-8pm Mon-Thu, to 10pm Fri & Sat, to 8pm Sun)

Shopping

Salamanca Market
MARKET

34 🔒 MAP P68, C7

Every Saturday since 1972, the open-air Salamanca Market has filled the tree-lined expanses of Salamanca Pl with more than 300 stalls. Fresh organic produce, secondhand clothes and books, tacky tourist souvenirs, ceramics and woodwork, cheap sunglasses,

Friday Night Fandango

Some of Hobart's best live tunes get an airing every Friday night at the Salamanca Arts Centre Courtyard (p59). It's a free community event with the adopted name 'Rektango'. Acts vary month to month – expect anything from African beats to rockabilly, folk and gypsy-Latino. Drinks essential (sangria in summer, mulled wine in winter); dancing near-essential.

antiques, exuberant buskers, quality food and drink...it's all here, but people-watching is the real name of the game.

A free shuttle bus runs between various stops in the city and the market every 10 minutes between 9am and 2pm (see the website for stop details). On foot, the market is around 10 minutes from the city centre.Rain or shine – don't miss it! (📞03-6238 2843; www.salamancamarket.com.au; Salamanca Pl; ⏰8am-3pm Sat)

Handmark Gallery ART

35 🔒 MAP P68, D7

A key tenant at the Salamanca Arts Centre (p70), Handmark has been here for 30 years, displaying unique ceramics, glass, woodwork and jewellery, plus paintings and sculpture – 100% Tasmanian, 100% exquisite.

Exhibitions change fortnightly or monthly. (📞03-6223 7895; www.handmark.com.au; 77 Salamanca Pl; ⏰10am-5pm Mon-Fri, to 4pm Sat & Sun)

Wursthaus Kitchen FOOD

36 🔒 MAP P68, B7

Follow your nose into this brilliant fine-food showcase just off Salamanca Place, selling cheeses, cakes, breads, olives, wines and pre-prepared meals. Oh, and amazing sausages! (📞03-6224 0644; www.wursthauskitchen.com.au; 1 Montpelier Retreat, Hobart; ⏰8.30am-6pm Mon-Fri, 8am-5pm Sat, 10am-5pm Sun)

Customs House Hotel (p65)

Hobart Book Shop BOOKS

37 🔒 MAP P68, C8

Step into the hushed Hobart Book Shop, with its excellent array of reads and dedicated wall full of Tasmanian authorly efforts. (📞03-6223 1803; www.hobartbookshop.com.au; 22 Salamanca Sq, Hobart; 🕙9am-6pm Mon-Fri, to 5pm Sat, 10am-5pm Sun)

Kathmandu SPORTS & OUTDOORS

38 🔒 MAP P68, C8

Gear up for your imminent Tasmanian bushwalking epic at this excellent outdoors shop, founded in the 1980s by latter-day Tasmanian Jan Cameron (who sold the business in 2006). Socks, boots, tents, thermal gear, gas cookers and more. (📞03-6224 3027; www.kathmandu.com.au; 16 Salamanca Sq, Hobart; 🕙9am-5.30pm Mon-Thu, to 7pm Fri, to 5pm Sat, 10am-4.30pm Sun)

Salamanca Market

If you're only going to be in Hobart for a few days, make sure one of them is a Saturday so you can check out Salamanca Market (p81), which has been filling trestle tables since 1972. Rain or shine it's an engaging experience, with as many things to eat and drink as buskers and things to buy. And unless you're going to get here at 6am, forget about finding a car park!

Art Mob ART

39 🔒 MAP P68, E2

Gorgeous (and ethically sourced) Aboriginal fine arts from around Australia have found their way to the Hobart waterfront. Packing and freight available. (📞03-6236 9200; www.artmob.com.au; 29 Hunter St, Hobart; 🕙10am-6pm)

Explore ⊛
Northern Hobart

Hobart's Northern suburbs are a real mix of tough working-class neighbourhoods and engaging cultural highlights. North Hobart itself is home to the city's most ebullient, bohemian restaurant and nightlife strip, strung along a sinewy stretch of Elizabeth St. Cafes, a cinema, pubs, craft-beer breweries, multicultural eats, live music venues – it's all here.

The Short List

○ **MONA (p102)** *Immersing yourself in this amazing museum.*

○ **North Hobart Restaurants (p96)** *Eating your way along Elizabeth St.*

○ **Royal Tasmanian Botanical Gardens (p93)** *Wandering through historic gardens.*

○ **Craft Beer Scene (p99)** *Sampling the product at breweries and pubs.*

○ **State Cinema (p101)** *Catching a flick at this plush art-house cinema.*

Getting There

🚗 Driving around North Hobart and the other northern suburbs is the easiest way to go.

🚗 Grab a cab to the North Hobart restaurants then back to your accommodation.

🚶 Explore the North Hobart strip on foot.

🚌 Route 551 runs from central Hobart to North Hobart.

Neighbourhood Map on p92

Royal Tasmanian Botanical Gardens (p93) MASTAPIECE/SHUTTERSTOCK ©

Top Experience 📷
Discover Trendy North Hobart

◉ MAP P92, B3

North Hobart (or 'NoHo' to those with a sense of humour), for decades one of Hobart's poorer suburbs, is now a hip enclave with soaring real-estate prices and new-found bohemian soul. The Elizabeth St strip sustains dozens of restaurants and at least one watering hole for every night of the week. Add Hobart's best cinema and live-music venue to the mix and you've got one seriously potent little neighbourhood.

Eating in NoHo

Hungry? Head straight to North Hobart. Bounded by Federal St to the North and Burnett St to the south, the buzzy 'NoHo' strip along Elizabeth St has something for all tastes, from a spiffy steakhouse grill to Indian, Italian, Asian, Thai, Mexican, Turkish, tapas, burger joints, kebab shops, bakeries, cafes, patisseries, espresso nooks...

The vibe here is relaxed and earthy, the antithesis of the flashier waterfront scene. Most restaurants here are BYO (bring-your-own alcoholic drinks, sometimes wine only), and you'll generally feel comfortable wearing jeans and a T-shirt. The scene is fast-changing: new businesses are opening all the time, steadily occupying new shops south of Burnett St as options diminish on the main strip. If you wanted tangible evidence of Hobart's emerging rep as a foodie haunt, here it is!

Time for a Drink?

In between all the North Hobart eateries you'll find a clutch of places to wet your whistle – some crammed with hipsters and savvy wine drinkers, some resolutely old-school and home to a species of old boozehound you don't see too often in Hobart these days.

Top spots for a drink include The Winston (p99), a scruffy craft-beer pub at the northern end of the strip; the Republic Bar & Café (p101) at the southern end (also Hobart's best live-music room); the wine bar Willing Bros (p100); and Room For A Pony (p100), a spacious former petrol station doing good things with local wine and spirits. And if you are into propping up the bar (or just read a lot of Charles Bukowski), ask someone to point you towards the Queen's Head or the Crescent Hotel.

★ Top Tips

○ Parking can be tight around Elizabeth St, but there's a big car park behind the stores off Burnett St (once servicing a now-closed neighbourhood supermarket).

○ Book ahead at most restaurants here: it's a popular precinct.

○ Running late and no time for a pre-movie drink? Don't fret: at the State Cinema (p101) you can take a glass of something good into the theatre with you.

✕ Take a Break

The North Hobart restaurant strip along Elizabeth St is one big break waiting to be taken. For coffee and cake the artful Sweet Envy (p95) is unbeatable.

For a crafty ale in the afternoon try the hipster-filled Winston (p99) pub.

Tangles

Legendary Australian cricketer and all-round good guy Max Walker (1948–2016), nicknamed 'Tangles' for his zany (but highly effective) bowling style, grew up in North Hobart. Max senior ran the big red-brick Empire Hotel – now the Republic Bar & Café (p101) – on the corner of Elizabeth and Burnett Sts, and Max junior was a regular interference underfoot at the bar. Aside from claiming 138 wickets in 34 international cricket test matches at an average of 27.47, Tangles was also a trained architect, a writer (14 books!), a TV presenter, public speaker, professional footballer (he played VFL football with the Melbourne Demons before he became a pro cricketer) and father of five kids. So raise a glass to Tangles – an irrepressible Tasmanian character – as you catch a live band at the Republic today.

Live Music

You can occasionally spy a sneaky busker twanging a guitar in the shadows here, but a more viable live-music option is the Republic Bar & Café. Formerly the staunch red-brick Empire Hotel, the Republic now hosts the pick of the Australian and international touring acts that visit Hobart (those not big enough to sell out a stadium), with local original acts filling out the gaps in the schedule. Great food and beer complete the package.

The Winston also has regular live music, as does the rangy Homestead bar (country, folk, blues and cheap beers), a little further down Elizabeth St.

Art-house Cinema

Feel like a flick? The plush State Cinema (p101) at the upper end of the Elizabeth St strip is an old-timey theatre (1913) that's been turned into an art-house miniplex, with eight snug screening rooms, a rooftop screen for nights when Hobart's weather gods are feeling charitable, plus a bar, a cafe, and the fabulous State Cinema Bookstore (p101), where the selection of books on art and cinema is predictably good.

Walking Tour 🥾

North Hobart Streetwise

The North Hobart strip – at its essence the 500m stretch of Elizabeth St between Federal St to the north and Burnett St to the south – has evolved over the past decade into Hobart's alternative food and drink hub. It's an effervescent place, night or day, with dozens of multicultural places to eat and a new breed of craft-beer and wine bars complimenting old-school pubs. Hobart's best cinema and live-music venue are here too.

Start Elizabeth St; bus stop 7, Elizabeth St

End Elizabeth St; bus stop 3, Elizabeth St

Length 1.5km; one hour

❶ North Hobart Post Office

What a beauty! A bright architectural spark at the top of the Elizabeth St strip, the ornate 1920s North Hobart Post Office is totally endearing. Painted handsomely in burgundy, cream and forest-green, it's a locally cherished building. It's enough to make you want to write a letter.

❷ Swan St

North Hobart was traditionally one of Hobart's edgier working-class enclaves – home to hard-drinking, hard-fisted hombres employed at the zinc factory at nearby Lutana. Some of the streets around here you'd probably avoid walking down, given the choice. Swan St was one such avenue: check out the gorgeous redbrick Victorian houses along its southern flank.

❸ North Hobart Pubs

North Hobart was complicit in the city's rampant booziness in colonial times, and despite the advent of craft beer, there are still some old-time pubs here. Try the **Queens Head Hotel** (400 Elizabeth St), hanging tough in the thick of the action; or the **Crescent Hotel** (100 Burnett St), around the corner.

❹ Hungry? Of Course You Are

Eating-out is North Hobart's *raison d'etre*. Walking down Elizabeth St you'll be spoilt for choice, with dozens of options vying for your hunger: Indian stalwarts, Mexican upstarts, Italian interlopers, brilliant bakeries and cool cafes.

❺ Little Arthur St

A little pedestrian alleyway runs west off Elizabeth St and becomes Little Arthur St, a photo-worthy laneway with some of North Hobart's oldest workers' cottages on one side, and (sadly) a car park and fat bank of ugly brown-brick 1980s townhouses on the other. Worth a look.

❻ South of Burnett St

A Western urban inevitability: suburbs gentrify, become hip, rents rise, and new businesses need to think laterally to get a foothold. So it is with North Hobart: but thinking outside the box, new restaurants, bars and cafes have seeded themselves south of Burnett St, extending the NoHo scene downhill. Sub-Burnett trailblazers include T-Bone Brewing Co (p99), Capulus Espresso (p100) and Amici Italian (p97).

❼ Shambles Brewery

In an un-obvious location midway between the main North Hobart action and the CBD is the excellent Shambles Brewery (p99). Shambles is notable for its slick interior design, excellent hoppy offerings and sense of humour (try the velvet-smooth Barry White porter).

Northern Hobart

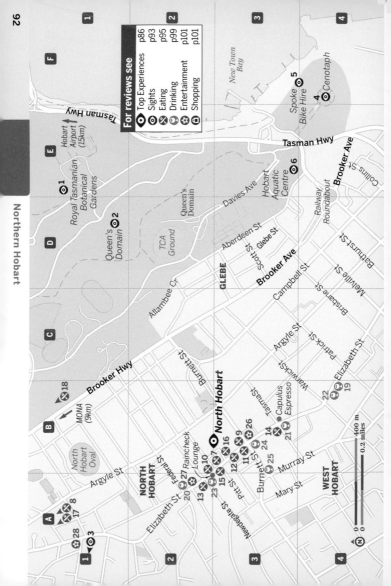

For reviews see

◈	Top Experiences	p86
◉	Sights	p93
⊗	Eating	p95
⬤	Drinking	p99
⊛	Entertainment	p101
⬠	Shopping	p101

Royal Tasmanian Botanical Gardens ◉1

Queen's Domain ◉2

Hobart Airport (15km) Tasman Hwy →

New Town Bay

Spoke ◉5 Bike Hire ◉4 Cenotaph

Tasman Hwy

Hobart Aquatic Centre ◉6

Brooker Ave

Queen's Domain

Davies Ave

TCA Ground

Allambee Cr

Aberdeen St

Glebe St

Scott St

GLEBE

Brooker Ave

Campbell St

Railway Roundabout

Collins St

Brisbane St

Melville St

Bathurst St

Patrick St

Argyle St

Warwick St

Brooker Hwy

MONA (9km) →

⊗18▲

North Hobart Oval

Argyle St

Burnett St

Elizabeth St

Federal St

Raincheck Lounge ⊛27

⊗20

⊗13

NORTH HOBART

◈ North Hobart

⊗23 ⬠10

Pitt St

Newdegate St

⊗15 ⊗7 ⬠16 ⊗12 ⊗11

⊗9 ⊗26 14 24

⊗25

Tasma St

Capulus Espresso

21

22 ⊗ 19

WEST HOBART

Burnett St

Murray St

Mary St

Elizabeth St

⊛28 ⊗8 ⊗17 ◉3 ⊗A1

400 m

0.2 miles

N

0

Sights

Royal Tasmanian Botanical Gardens
GARDENS

1 MAP P92, E1

On the eastern side of the Queen's Domain park, these beguiling 200-year-old gardens feature more than 6000 exotic and native plant species. Picnic on the lawns, check out the Subantarctic House or grab a bite at the restaurant or cafe. Call to ask about guided tours. Down the hill from the main entrance, opposite Government House, is the site of the **former Beaumaris Zoo**, where the last captive Tasmanian tiger died in 1936; a couple of dilapidated enclosures remain. (☏03-6166 0451; www.rtbg.tas.gov.au; Lower Domain Rd, Queen's Domain; admission free; ⏲8am-6.30pm Oct-Mar, to 5.30pm Apr & Sep, to 5pm May-Aug)

Queen's Domain
PARK

2 MAP P92, D1

In Hobart's early days, the leafy hill on the city's northern side became the governor's private playground, upon which no houses were to be built. Today the hillock is called the Queen's Domain and is public parkland, strewn with cricket, tennis and athletics centres, the Hobart Aquatic Centre (p94), native grasslands, lookouts, the Cenotaph (p94) and the Royal Tasmanian Botanical Gardens. Pedestrian overpasses on the western side provide easy access to North Hobart. (☏03-6238 2886; www.hobartcity.com.au; via Tasman Hwy, Glebe)

Royal Tasmanian Botanical Gardens

LKONYA/SHUTTERSTOCK ©

Northern Hobart Sights

Urban Greenery 🌹

Hobart's Northern suburbs can feel a bit hard-edged and bleak at times. For a leafy antidote, stretch your legs with Hobart's lunchtime jogging crew around the wide-open Cenotaph (p94) and hilly Queen's Domain (p93), or tag along with local pram-pushing families on a wander through the lush nooks and rolling riverside lawns of the Royal Tasmanian Botanical Gardens (p93).

Lady Franklin Gallery   GALLERY

3 ⊙ MAP P92, A1

In an exquisitely proportioned colonnaded 1842 sandstone building called Ancanthe (Greek for 'vale of flowers' – enough of a reason to visit alone), the gorgeous Lady Franklin Gallery displays contemporary work by Tasmanian artists. To get here without your own wheels, take bus 551, 552 or 553. (📞 03-6228 0076; www.artstas. com.au/our-history/lady-franklin-gallery; Ancanthe Park, 268 Lenah Valley Rd, Lenah Valley; admission free; 🕐 11am-4pm Sat & Sun)

Cenotaph   MONUMENT

4 ⊙ MAP P92, F4

Part of the broader Queen's Domain, the epic Cenotaph monument forms a visual finishing point if you look down the *looong* axis of Macquarie St from South Hobart. It's actually a war memorial: there used to be soccer pitches mowed into the grass around its base, but things are a bit more respectful these days. In 1841 the Queens Battery was built here, with guns trained towards any menace from the sea. (📞 03-6238 2886; www.hobartcity.com.au; off McVilly Dr, Glebe)

Spoke Bike Hire   CYCLING

5 ⊙ MAP P92, F3

Mountain bikes, hybrids and kids' bikes for hire, plus loads of advice on riding around the city and beyond. You can hop on the bike track here and roll all the way to MONA (about 20km). (📞 03-6232 4848; www.spokebikehire.com.au; 20 McVilly Dr, Cenotaph; bike hire per hr/day/2 days from $15/25/45; 🕐 9am-5pm Sep-May, shorter hours Jun-Aug)

Hobart Aquatic Centre   SWIMMING

6 ⊙ MAP P92, E3

The excellent Hobart Aquatic Centre at the foot of the Queen's Domain (officially the 'Doone Kennedy Hobart Aquatic Centre', named after a former mayor) has a leisure pools, lap-swimming pools, a spa, a sauna, a steam room, gym, aqua aerobics, and regular aerobics for landlubbers. (📞 03-6222 6999; www.hobartcity.com. au/community/doone-kennedy-hobart-aquatic-centre; 1 Davies Ave, Glebe; adult/child/family $8/5/20; 🕐 6am-9pm Mon-Fri, 8am-6pm Sat & Sun)

Eating

Burger Haus
BURGERS $

Boasting big beefy burgers, a little outdoor terrace, craft beers and ciders, and a view that combines a concrete car park with the moody hues of kunanyi/Mt Wellington, this back-lane burger bar has it all (see **12**  Map p92, B3) ! The Haus Burger (with bacon, onion rings, caramelised pineapple and mustard mayo) reigns supreme. (📞03-6234 9507; www.theburgerhaus. com.au; 364a Elizabeth St, North Hobart; burgers $13-16; ⏱11.30am-late)

Sweet Envy
PATISSERIE, CAFE $

7 🍴 MAP P92, B3

A delicate diversion along North Hobart's restaurant strip, Sweet Envy conjures up gossamer-light macarons, madeleines and cupcakes, plus gourmet pies and sausage rolls (try the pork and fennel version) and fantastic ice creams and sorbets, all made on the premises. Grab a scoop of badass 'Darth Vader' super-choc ice cream and hit the streets. (📞03-6234 8805; www.sweetenvy. com; 341 Elizabeth St, North Hobart; items $5-10; ⏱8.30am-5pm Tue-Sat)

Myu
ASIAN $$

8 🍴 MAP P92, A1

Let yourself in on a Hobart secret at this unsigned, unadulterated dining room in an unprepossessing strip of shops where the ever-changing menu rolls straight off the home printer each night. Expect a pan-Asian journey – the night's menu might include beef rendang, Hainanese chicken, bao

Northern Hobart Eating

Sweet Envy

SWEET ENVY ©

and momos. (☏03-6228 7777; www.
facebook.com/Myu.easybites; 2/93
New Town Rd, New Town; mains $19-28;
⏱5.30-8.30pm Tue-Sat)

Annapurna
INDIAN $$

9 MAP P92, B3

It seems like half of Hobart lists
modest Annapurna as their
favourite eatery (you'd better
book). Northern and southern
Indian options are served with
absolute proficiency: the *masala
dosa* (south Indian crepe filled
with curried potato) is a crowd
favourite. Takeaway and good-
value group banquets available.
Hard to top. (☏03-6236 9500; www.
annapurnaindiancuisine.com; 305
Elizabeth St, North Hobart; mains $16-
26, banquets $25-34; ⏱5-10pm; ✎)

Vanidol's
ASIAN $$

10 MAP P92, B2

A pioneering North Hobart
restaurant, Vanidol's has a diverse
menu that travels effortlessly
around Asia with dishes including
spicy Thai beef salad, Nepalese
lamb curry and Balinese chicken.
Expect a well-thumbed passport
full of vegetarian dishes, too. Also
in South Hobart (p121). (☏03-6234
9307; www.vanidols-north-hobart.com;
353 Elizabeth St, North Hobart; mains
$18-27; ⏱5.30pm-late, closed Mon
Jun-Aug; ✎)

Veg Bar
VEGETARIAN $$

11 MAP P92, B3

'Plant-based eatery' may be a
coded way of saying 'vegetarian
joint', but there's really no need

State Bookstore (p101)

IMAGE SUPPLIED BY STATE CINEMA ©

for disguises. Veg Bar is a quality outfit, from the snappy design (swing seats, polished concrete, faux-turf wall) to the menu of veg classics (kimchi fried rice, massaman curry) and wholesome burgers, wraps and bowls – all organic and local. Beer, wine and cocktails, too. (☑03-6231 1593; www.vegbar.com.au; 346 Elizabeth St, North Hobart; mains $14-23; ☺11.30am-9pm; ☑)

Capital ITALIAN $$

12 ☒ MAP P92, B3

Authentic Italian pizza, pasta and *dolci* (dessert) in the thick of the Elizabeth St action – an experience made even better by one of Hobart's best interiors (think pressed tin, rusted steel, polished concrete and wreathes of dried chillis; the owners did it themselves – talented!). Try the porcini mushroom gnocchi with three-cheese sauce, or the Calabrese salami pizza. Always busy – a good sign. (☑03-6231 1101; www.capitalrestaurant.com.au; 364 Elizabeth St, North Hobart; mains $24-38; ☺5-10pm Mon-Wed, 11.30am-10pm Thu-Sun)

Born in Brunswick CAFE $$

13 ☒ MAP P92, A2

Born in Brunswick is a stylistically elevated Hobart cafe (blond timbers, huge colourful bird murals and white everywhere else) with a creative menu of all-day offerings (coffee-and-cake takes on a new meaning when the 'cake' is blood lime and macadamia cheesecake with honeycomb). Try the house-smoked Huon salmon with crispy egg, black sesame and Tasmanian wasabi. It's all quite impressive. (www.borninbrunswick.com.au; 410 Elizabeth St, North Hobart; mains $14-24; ☺8am-3pm Tue-Sun)

Amici Italian ITALIAN $$

14 ☒ MAP P92, B3

Mighty fine pasta, calzones and pizzas in a corner-shop restaurant that manages to feel more sophisticated than the menu, which still feels compelled to include an 'Aussie' pizza and a dedicated 'gourmet pizza' section (admittedly, very nice). The fettuccine marinara is hard to beat. (☑03-6234 7973; www.amicirestaurant.net.au; 310 Elizabeth St, North Hobart; mains $18-36; ☺5-10pm Tue-Sat, to 9pm Sun)

Pancho Villa MEXICAN $$

15 ☒ MAP P92, B3

A red-brick bank turned super-moody tequila bar and restaurant with Day of the Dead skulls, pressed metal lanterns and stained-glass windows – it's like stepping into a Gothic novel. Choose from creative tacos, quesadillas and BBQ jerk chicken (with churros dulce de leche to sweeten the finish), with 40 tequilas to fire things up.

Find the secret bookshelf doorway to the courtyard **Voodoo Bar** for a hit of eight ball, bar snacks and a whole lot more

Trailblazing Cafe

🍴🍽️

A trailblazing North Hobart cafe (here long before all the hype), **Raincheck Lounge** (Map p92, A2; 📞 03-6234 5975; www.rainchecklounge. com.au; 392 Elizabeth St, North Hobart; breakfast mains $15-22, lunch & dinner tapas $6-16; ⏰7am-6pm Sun-Tue, to 10pm Wed-Sat) is an enduring slice of urban cool. Raincheck's bohemian room and street-side tables see punters sipping coffee, reconstituting over big breakfasts, and conversing over generous tapas such as broccolini with anchovy crumb, or chorizo in peperonata. There's a decent wine list and sassy staff to boot.

tequila. (📞03-6234 4161; www. panchovilla.com.au; cnr Elizabeth & Pitt Sts, North Hobart; small plates $16-25, large plates $26-38; ⏰5.30pm-late)

All Thai

THAI $$

16 🍴 MAP P92, B3

Straight-up, reliable Thai offerings on the North Hobart strip – orange-and-black colour scheme, clattery chairs and a busy vibe. Check the blackboard for daily specials. (📞03-6234 8113; www. allthai.com.au; 333 Elizabeth St, North Hobart; mains $16-24; ⏰5.30-9pm Sun-Thu, to 9.30pm Fri & Sat; 🌱)

Kalbi

KOREAN $$

Sick of too-subtle Japanese and predictable Chinese? Kalbi (see 23 ⦿ Map p92, A2) offers keenly priced Korean on the Elizabeth St strip, its minimalist approach to interior design offset by sheets of Korean newspaper entirely covering one wall. Order a *bi bim bap* – a traditional Korean bowl of spicy sauce with beef, pork, tofu or barbecue chicken.

(📞03-6236 9725; www.facebook. com/kalbinorthhobart; 396a Elizabeth St, North Hobart; mains $14-18; ⏰11.30am-2.30pm Tue-Sat, 5-9pm Tue-Sun)

Ragazzi & Co

PIZZA $$

Down a sneaky alleyway off Elizabath St, Ragazzi & Co (see 12 ⦿ Map p92, B3) is a takeaway pizza hole-in-the-wall, doing a roaring trade every night. The Caligula (prosciutto, chilli, tomato, basil, black olives and Parmesan) is a show-stopper. Basic pastas also available. (📞03-6234 9611; www. facebook.com/ragazziandco; rear 364 Elizabeth St, North Hobart; pizzas $13-21; ⏰4.30-9.30pm)

Roaring Grill

STEAK $$$

Beefing up the offerings in NoHo is this sassy steakhouse (see 9 ⦿ Map p92, B3) named for the Roaring Forties winds that wash and dry Tasmania. It's a stylish split-level fit-out – exposed brickwork, dark-wood tables and globular glassware – with the usual cuts (eye fillet, scotch fillet, rib eye, fillet mignon) done well rather than well done. Also serves up fish, ceviche and oysters. (☏03-6231 1301; www.roaringgrill.com; 301 Elizabeth St, North Hobart; mains $26-60; ⏱5pm-late Mon & Tue, from noon Wed-Sun)

Lebrina   MODERN AUSTRALIAN $$$

17 ✕ MAP P92, A1

Foodies and critics alike enthuse about Lebrina. Concealed in Hobart's northern reaches, it looks small and unremarkable from the outside, but inside it's sheer dining pleasure, from the decor to the flawless service to the wine list and, of course, the creative Mod Oz offerings. Bookings mandatory. (☏03-6228 7775; www.lebrina.com; 155 New Town Rd, New Town; mains $49.50; ⏱6.30-9pm Tue-Sat)

Cornelian Bay Boat House   MODERN AUSTRALIAN $$$

18 ✕ MAP P92, B1

About 3km north of the city, this stylish, light-filled restaurant-bar occupies a converted beach pavilion on shallow Cornelian Bay – the swimming destination of choice for sweaty Hobartians circa 1900. The menu is highly evolved, starring quality local produce and delivered with super service. Try the Boat House chowder or the Scottsdale pork loin with smoked pineapple and cider-and-sage jelly. (☏03-6228 9289; www.theboathouse.com.au; Queen's Walk, Cornelian Bay; mains $29-38; ⏱noon-2pm daily, 6-8.30pm Wed-Sat)

Drinking

Shambles Brewery   CRAFT BEER

19 🚇 MAP P92, B4

An excellent brewery just south of the NoHo strip, with minimalist interiors and a concrete-block bar. Head out the back to drink among the vats (and try the table tennis). Tasting paddles are $14, or refill your 'growler' (1.9L bottle) to take home and savour. Terrific beery bar food too: burgers, fried chicken and the like. Try the Dirty Copper amber ale. (☏03-6289 5639; www.shamblesbrewery.com.au; 222 Elizabeth St, North Hobart; ⏱4pm-late Wed & Thu, from noon Fri-Sun)

The Winston   PUB

20 🚇 MAP P92, A2

The Winston is a craft-beery, US-style alehouse. Grab a pint of the house stout from one of the beardy guys behind the bar and check out the wall of US registration plates near the pool table. The food flavours – buffalo wings, grilled corn, brisket – match the setting. (☏03-6231 2299; www.thewinstonbar.com; 381 Elizabeth St, North Hobart; ⏱4pm-late)

T-Bone Brewing Co   CRAFT BEER

21 🚇 MAP P92, B3

Obsessively brewed real ales steal the show at this new North Hobart brew-bar, a stylish black beer-bunker reviving an old corner shop, near the Elizabeth St action. Sit by the fold-back windows, or

New Coffee Cool

Hobart's streets sustain a hip new breed of pop-up coffee carts and hole-in-the-wall coffee shops. In North Hobart, you can get a slice of tart, a bit of cake or a biscuit at low-tech **Capulus Espresso** (Map p92, B3; ☏0459 661 001; www.facebook.com/capulusespresso; 271 Elizabeth St, North Hobart; items from $3; ☺6am-4pm Mon-Fri, to noon Sat), a coffee nook behind a roller door just south of the NoHo strip. But what you're really here for is the coffee – outstanding hot black stuff. Check out the kooky hairdresser through the back door.

play peek-a-boo with the beer vats, bubbling beyond a hole in the wall. Tasting flights $16. (☏0407 502 521; www.tbonebrewing.com.au; 308 Elizabeth St, North Hobart; ☺4pm-late Wed & Thu, 2pm-late Fri-Sun)

Bar Wa Izakaya
COCKTAIL BAR

22 🚇 MAP P92, B4

Backed by glowing shelves of whisky tumblers, Bar Wa Izakaya is a atmospheric Japanese bar with more sake, Sapporo and Japanese whisky on offer than seems plausible. Order a plate of tempura mushrooms or kingfish sashimi (bar food $6 to $16) to temper your whisky tasting flight. (☏03-6288 7876; www.facebook.com/barwaizakaya; 216-218 Elizabeth St, Hobart; ☺noon-midnight)

Willing Bros
WINE BAR

23 🚇 MAP P92, A2

This wine bar is NoHo's most sophisticated resident. Pull up a window seat at the front of the skinny room and sip something hip from the tightly edited menu of reds, whites and bubbles. Food drifts from goat curd ravioli to bangers and mash. (☏03-6234 3053; www.facebook.com/willingbros; 390 Elizabeth St, North Hobart; ☺3pm-late Tue-Sun)

Room For A Pony
BAR

24 🚇 MAP P92, B3

There's more than enough room for a pony at this converted petrol station – you could fit a whole herd on the fake-grass terrace out the front. Stop by for a Chinese fried chilli omelette or a burger (mains $11 to $20), a glass of wine, or a local-spirits cocktail on the deck (the rhubarb sour is a killer). (☏03-6231 0508; www.roomforapony.com.au; 338 Elizabeth St, North Hobart; ☺7am-3.30pm Mon & Tue, to midnight Wed-Fri, 8am-midnight Sat & Sun)

Crescent Hotel
PUB

25 🚇 MAP P92, B3

The architecture falls on to the ye-olde mock-Tudor column on the ledger, but as far as Hobart pubs go, the Crescent is as earthy and unpretentious as the get. It's a sit-on-a-stool-at-11am-and-talk-to-the-barman kinda joint. Big pub meals (mains $10 to $34) and occasional live bands, too. (📞0447 090 870; www.facebook.com/crescenthotelhobart; 100 Burnett St, North Hobart; ⏱11am-9pm Tue-Sat)

Entertainment

Republic Bar & Café   LIVE MUSIC

26 ⭐ MAP P92, B3

The Republic is a raucous art-deco pub hosting live music every night (often with free entry). It's the number-one live-music pub around town, with an always interesting line-up, including international acts. Loads of different beers andp excellent food (mains $20 to $33; try the Jack Daniel's–marinated rump steak). Just the kind of place you'd love to call your local. (📞03-6234 6954; www.republicbar.com.au; 299 Elizabeth St, North Hobart; ⏱3pm-late Mon & Tue, from noon Wed-Sun; 📶)

State Cinema   CINEMA

27 ⭐ MAP P92, A2

Saved from the wrecking ball in the 1980s, the 11-screen State shows independent and art-house flicks. There's a great cafe and bar on-site, plus a summertime rooftop screen (with another bar!), a browse-worthy bookshop and the foodie temptations of North Hobart's restaurants right outside.

The cinema dates back to 1913 when it opened as one of Tasmania's first purpose-built picture houses. Economic rises and falls saw the old State close and dodge demolition several times, before finally closing in 2002, only to be revived in 2005. (📞03-6234 6318; www.statecinema.com.au; 375 Elizabeth St, North Hobart; tickets adult/child $20/16)

Jokers Comedy Club   COMEDY

28 ⭐ MAP P92, A1

Live weekly stand-up comedy at Hobart's Polish Club, just north of the main North Hobart strip. Cheap drinks and big laughs from Australian and overseas comics. (📞0427 726 123; www.jokerscomedy.com.au; Polish Corner, cnr New Town & Augusta Rds, New Town; tickets $23-25; ⏱shows 8pm Wed, bar from 7.30pm)

Shopping

State Bookstore   BOOKS

Usually the movie is adapted from the book, but in this case the bookshop is adapted from the adjoining State Cinema (see 27 ⭐ Map p92, A2). Recently relocated into a larger space, its mainstays are art, architecture, literary fiction and high-quality cookbooks – all the good things. (📞03-6169 0720; www.statecinemabookstore.com.au; 377 Elizabeth St, North Hobart; ⏱9.30am-7pm Sun & Mon, to 9pm Tue-Sat)

Worth a Trip 🔭
Experience the Extraordinary MONA

MONA – the brilliant, notorious, challenging Museum of Old & New Art in Hobart's northern suburbs – is a very unusual place, and not just because it's founded/funded by an eccentric gambling millionaire. It's also more fabulously unhinged, sexy, renegade, offbeat, puerile and intelligent than any other art museum you might care to mention. Look, feel and think: that's the MONA effect.

Museum of Old & New Art
☎ 03-6277 9900
www.mona.net.au
655 Main Rd, Berriedale
adult/child $28/free, Tasmanian residents free
🕙 10am-6pm Jan, 10am-6pm Wed-Mon Feb-Apr & Dec, to 5pm Wed-Mon May-Nov

Monanism

'Monanism' is the name given to the broad collection of art here, numbering upwards of 1900 pieces. Not all of these are on display, but works are rotated regularly to keep things (more) interesting. Some works are so big and/or important that the museum was designed around them, including *Snake*, a 46m-long array of images exploring the connections between myth and modernity; and the *Chamber of Pausiris,* containing the coffin and mummy of a 2000-year-old Egyptian.

Other must-sees include the room dedicated solely to the worship of Madonna; the fabulous *bit.fall,* a programmed waterfall that spells out words as it descends; and every kid's favourite, the impressive poo machine *Cloaca Professional,* which recreates (with alarmingly accurate waste products) the human digestive system.

For an insight into MONA's incredible architecture, check out www.mona.net.au/museum/architecture – an entertaining interview with the architects, explaining the thinking behind the design and the rather amazing site.

The O

At MONA there aren't any plaques on walls or dimly lit pasted-up A4 explanations of what you're looking at. And it is dimly lit in here! You're going to need some kind of guide to get you through.

The solution is 'The O' – essentially an iPod with headphones, issued for free, loaded-up with all kinds of art info that you can either listen to and accept, read and forget, or dismiss outright. Content is classified into 'Art Wank', 'Gonzo', 'Ideas' and 'Interviews', putting various spins on what you're seeing, including (often hilarious) commentary from David Walsh and the artists themselves.

★ Top Tips

◦ Some of the stuff at MONA is...well, pervy. If you blush easily, ask which naughty rooms to avoid. Ditto if you're strobe-averse.

◦ MONA is open every day in January (the rest of the year, Tuesday is staff sleep-in day).

◦ If you're from Tasmania, admission is free (bring ID).

✕ Take a Break

Grab a coffee and quick-fire bite at the museum cafe, or for a more refined experience, try the **Source** (☏03-6277 9904; www.mona.net. au/eat-drink/the-source-restaurant; mains $22-40; ⊗7.30-10am & noon-2pm Wed-Mon, 6pm-late Fri & Sat) restaurant.

★ Getting There

Ferry MR-1 from Brooke Street Pier

Car Via Brooker Hwy (11km)

Bus MONA shuttle bus from the city or airport

Bicycle 20km from the city

The O is also interactive – hit the 'love' or 'hate' icons to give a little vox-pop feedback. If you want to use your own iPhone you can download The O app (free wi-fi at the museum). Afterwards, you can have the details of your visit (as recorded by The O) emailed to you, so you can relive your MONA experience at home.

Exhibitions

As well as the main Monanism collection, MONA also hosts regular exhibitions digging up the dirt on specific subjects. In 2016 there was 'Hound in the Hunt', an experimental installation by artist Tim Jenison involving a distressingly simple method of recreating 17th-century art with mirrors; and 'On the Origin of Art', exploring how art, like the desire for food, sex or to protect our children, is hard-wired into our biology. Exhibitions cost extra, as you'd expect; book online.

Moorilla & Moo Brew

Before there was MONA, there was **Moorilla** (✆03-6277 9960; www. moorilla.com.au; tastings/tours $10/20; ⊘tastings 9.30am-5pm Mon-Wed, tours 3.30pm Wed-Mon), a winery started in 1962 by Claudio Alcorso (1913–2000), an Italian with a keen eye for

Ferry to MONA

MONA Goes Gothic

When the winter solstice creaks around in June, **Dark MOFO** (www.darkmofo.net.au; ⏰ Jun) stirs in the half-light. This moody festival – featuring live music, installations, readings, film noir and midnight feasts, all tapping into Hobart's edgy gothic undercurrents – has grown in popularity to rival the city's long-running New Year's festival scene. Locals rug-up, drink red wine around bonfires, talk, argue and eat, ruminating over the macabre and the unexpected.

Much less disquieting is the summertime **MONA FOMA** (Museum of Old & New Art Festival of Music & Art; www.mofo.net.au; ⏰ Jan), MONA's Festival of Music & Art, featuring eclectic musical offerings curated by a high-profile 'Eminent Artist in Residence' (EAR). Previous EARs have included John Cale, Ava Mendoza and Nick Cave. Stirring stuff.

architecture and an even better eye for a good grape. Now MONA runs Moorilla: you can taste some at the cellar door, drink some at the on-site bars and restaurants, or take a winery tour at 3.30pm Wednesday to Monday ($15, bookings essential).

MONA's **Moo Brew** (📞 03-6277 9900; www.moobrew.com.au; 76a Cove Hill Rd, Bridgewater; $15; ⏰ tours 12.45pm Fri) has been around since Hobart's hipsters were beardless and too young to obsess about craft beer. Quality offerings include a pilsner, hefeweizen, dark ale and pale ale, brewed in nearby Bridgewater. As with the Moorilla wines, you can taste some at MONA's cellar door, drink some on-site, or take a one-hour tour out at the brewery, starting every Friday at 12.45pm ($15; bookings required).

Bonus MONA

MONA is enough of a tourist lure in itself...but wait, there's more!

After swanning through the exhibits inside MONA, check out the excellent little **MONA Shop** (⏰ 10am-6pm daily Jan, 10am-6pm Wed-Mon Feb-Apr & Dec, 10am-5pm Wed-Mon May-Nov) near the entry, selling quirky, interesting and disarming gifts for the folks back home, plus excellent art books (pick up a copy of *A Bone of Fact*, the hefty 2014 autobiography of cashed-up MONA founder David Walsh).

Finally, for a slice of luxury, book one of the private, uber-chic **MONA Pavilions** (📞 03-6277 9911; www.mona.net.au/stay/mona-pavilions; d from $750; 🅿 ❄ 🛜 🏊). These eight modern, self-contained chalets (one- and two-bedroom) are equipped to the nines, with private balconies, wine cellars, river views and oh-so-discreet service. An indoor swimming pool is an essential aid to relaxation, and MONA itself is in your backyard.

Explore ✦

Battery Point, Sandy Bay & South Hobart

This broad southern swath is backed by looming Mt Wellington (kunanyi to the Muwinina people), the Battery Point headland jutting into the Derwent River. Battery Point was Hobart's first 'neighbourhood' and today hosts a photogenic clutch of old houses, cafes and B&Bs. Next door is affluent Sandy Bay, with atmospheric South Hobart nooked in below the mountain: both have excellent eateries.

The Short List

○ **kunanyi/Mt Wellington (p136)** *Driving to the summit of kunanyi.*

○ **Cascade Brewery (p128)** *Sipping ales and touring this legendary brewery.*

○ **Battery Point (p108)** *Exploring the area's historic streetscapes.*

○ **Cascades Female Factory Historic Site (p132)** *Understanding the ordeals of Hobart's female convicts.*

○ **Roaring 40s Kayaking (p118)** *Paddling a kayak around the waterfront.*

Getting There

🚗 BYO car is the way to go (though Battery Point parking is hellish).

🚶 Walk to Battery Point from the city or Salamanca Place.

🚌 For Sandy Bay take bus 402 or 429 from the city. For South Hobart, bus 446, 447, 448 or 449.

Neighbourhood Map on p116

Summit, kunanyi/Mt Wellington (p136) TERRY SZE/SHUTTERSTOCK ©

Top Experience 📷

Explore Maritime History at Battery Point

The old maritime village of Battery Point is a tight nest of lanes and 19th-century cottages. This harbourside 'hood oozes history, and a visit here is a window into Hobart's colonial soul. Having first been designated as farm land, Battery Point was soon rezoned as residential and hundreds of little sailors' and whalers' cottages sprang up. Today, cafes, galleries and B&Bs prevail.

◉ MAP P116, E2

Historic Highlights

Take a walk down **Kelly St** for a good look at some traditional, working-class Battery Point cottages; then spin around **Arthur Circus** – a sweet little circular street around a village green with a chestnut tree and a set of swings in it (pictured p110). The brick cottages here are typical of early Battery Point, built for soldiers from the local garrison. More affluent Battery Point mansions pop up along **Mona St** and the lower end of **Hampden Rd**.

You wouldn't know it these days, but Battery Point's residents didn't always maintain impeccable standards of behaviour (rum, sailors and prostitutes – what could possibly go wrong?). When the time came to repent, St George's Anglican Church (p117) on Cromwell St was the place to be. Designed by colonial architect John Lee Archer, this noble spire (1838) sits atop the highest point of the neighbourhood like a candle on a cake, and is visible from right across southern Hobart. It also served as a beacon for returning sailors, navigating their way up the misty Derwent River estuary.

For a condensed and highly authentic window into colonial life, pay a visit to Narryna Heritage Museum (p117) on Hampden Rd. This 1837 sandstone house is crammed with domestic remnants form Battery Point's early days.

Hampden Rd Scene

If Battery Point has a 'spine', Hampden Rd is it, a slender, sinewy thoroughfare that runs the length of the suburb, linking Sandy Bay Rd at one end with Castray Esplanade at the other. Along its length are most of Battery Point's commercial endeavours, including some good accommodation, a pub, a museum, some gift shops and some excellent cafes and restaurants. If you're out exploring the 'hood for a day, you'll probably find yourself drawn back here a couple of times for a coffee, some lunch

★ Top Tips

o Aside from some good restaurants, there's not much shakin' in Battery Point after dark. Plan on retreating to Salamanca Place.

o Parking here is as bad as it gets in Hobart: tight little streets with no driveways are a bad combo for drivers. Ditch the wheels and walk instead.

✕ Take a Break

Hampden Rd sustains a string of good cafes and restaurants: Jackman & McRoss (p118) is surely Hobart's best bakery-cafe.

For a sneaky drink, head to the hidden-away Shipwright's Arms Hotel (p124) on Colville St, with its timeless sea-going vibes.

or an afternoon glass of wine. Top of your list should be Jackman & McRoss (p118), a brilliant bakery-cafe that few would argue is Hobart's best; Ristorante Da Angelo (p120) for an early pizza dinner; and Magic Curries (p121), purveyors of Hobart's best Indian offerings.

Fancy a Beer?

Just off Hampden Rd at the Sandy Bay Rd end is Preachers (p124), a nooked-away bar in a historic cottage, with a laid-back beer garden. One of Hobart's first purveyors of fine craft beer, it's an eccentric spot for a cold one... and even has a ghost!. The **Prince of Wales Hotel** (📞 03-6223 6355; www.princeofwaleshotel.net.au; 55 Hampden Rd; d/q/f incl breakfast from $120/200/250; P 🤶), a short walk away on the corner of Hampden Rd and Kelly St, is a 1960s red-brick incursion, incongruously modernist in its design, but old enough now to invoke a certain sense of nostalgia.

Hidden Battery Point

Walking around Battery Point, it's often the little hidden places and surprising things that beguile and endear. You'll indeed need to be goat-like to traverse **Billy Goat Lane** and **Nanny Goat Lane** – steep, skinny flights of steps linking Quayle St with St Georges Tce on the Sandy Bay side of the suburb.

Another hidden gem is the little waterside **Purdon Featherstone Reserve** off Derwent Lane at

Where's the Battery?

The suburb's namesake gun battery was built in 1818 on the promontory overlooking the Derwent River, cannons aimed out towards prospective invading Americans, Russians, French, Dutch or whomever else might have had the gall to attack old Hobart Town and claim it as their own. The invasion never happened, the guns were dismantled and the site of the old battery – in Princes Park on the end of Hampden Rd – is now interred beneath a kids' playground.

the foot of Trumpeter St, named after some local boat builders. From here you can view Battery Point's last remaining boat yards and moorings. The unusual contemporary house on the right as you descend to the park was built for the founder of Incat (International Catmarans) – a latter-day Hobart boat-building success story.

Sometimes it's the more transient occurrences in Battery Point that give the neighbourhood its character: a little pile of seashells on a doorstep; gentle little river waves splashing onto the tiny beach at the bottom of Finlay St; the stencil graffiti poem on the wall of the Shipwright's Arms Hotel, which reads: *'Three flag-swept days/Ships monstrous and transitory/Heroes I could not captain'.*

Walking Tour 🥾

Battery Point Backstreets

Time-travel back into Hobart's colonial history with a walk around Battery Point. This was where the city's first farm was established, followed by military installations (the 'battery'), rows of compact sailors' cottages and estimable mansions built for wealthy merchants. History is everywhere here: a few hours exploring the backstreets is time well spent.

Start Hampden Rd; bus stop 5, Sandy Bay Rd

End Kelly's Steps; bus stop 5, Sandy Bay Rd

Length 2.5km; two hours

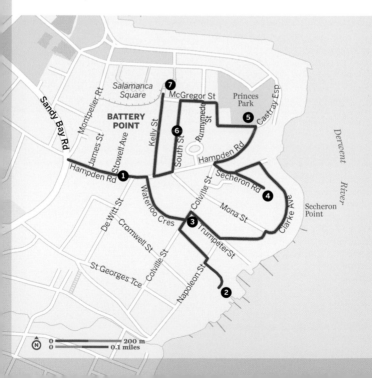

❶ Hampden Rd Cafes

Don't attempt anything without coffee and pastries. From Sandy Bay Rd, walk down Hampden Rd, Battery Point's photo-worthy commercial strip, and check yourself into one of the cafes here. Pull up a footpath table, get a feel for the village atmosphere and fuel-up for your walk ahead.

❷ Battery Point Shipyards

It's something of a surprise to discover that Battery Point still has working shipyards, congregating around the lower end of Napoleon St. Follow the arc of Waterloo Cres, cross Colville St and dogleg down Sloane St. Cast an eye over proceedings from the lovely little **Napoleon St Playground**.

❸ Shipwright's Arms Hotel

From Napoleon St, walk back up to Colville St where you'll find one of the sources of Battery Point's traditionally boozy rep – the old Shipwright's Arms Hotel (p124), which has been serving beers to seagoing types since 1846. Check out the maritime paraphernalia on the walls.

❹ Secheron House

Walk down Trumpeter St, turn left onto Marine Tce then cast an eye up Mona St to see some of Battery Point's more impressive houses. Follow Clarke Ave around to Secheron Rd, where the National Trust–listed Secheron House (1831) resides in colonial splendour – the most lovely of Battery Point's heritage mansions. Peek through the gates: it's a private home these days.

❺ Princes Park

Back on Hampden Rd, head downhill to Princes Park, where Battery Point's 'battery' once stood – a gun installation built in 1818 to protect Hobart from the threat of invading warships crewed by rival Europan powers. Princes Park is now perfectly peaceful...although you can still see the stone entrance to the old magazine (ammunition storage area) under the park.

❻ South St

Compact little South St has an inexplicably good vibe. In itself the street is unremarkable – a lane-like thoroughfare crowded with old timber and stone cottages that aren't particularly consistent or in particularly good condition. But South St oozes charm.

❼ Kelly's Steps

At the bottom of Kelly St are **Kelly's Steps**, named after one-time Hobart harbourmaster James Kelly. Built in 1839, the steps traverse the quarry face between Battery Point and Salamanca Place, which until their construction was impassable. From here the Salamanca Place bars are a short hop away – toast your Battery Point tour with a cold one or three.

Walking Tour 🥾

Hobart Pub Crawl

Some cities in the world are great drinking cities, and some cities aren't. Lucky for you, Hobart falls squarely into the former category – a hard-drinking town that's been three sheets to the wind since the days of rum-addled soldiers in the barracks and sea-soaked whalers in the waterfront pubs. Many of the town's most atmospheric old boozers are still here.

Start New Sydney Hotel

Finish Shipwright's Arms Hotel

Length 2.5km; five hours

❶ Take a Break

Nothing goes together quite as well as beer and pizza. Well, beer and curry, maybe... But for a fab Italian disc nearing the end of your pub crawl, try Battery Point's Ristorante Da Angelo (p120).

❷ New Sydney Hotel

You have to applaud the confidence: Hobart's colonists may have viewed their city as the new version of Sydney, but it was never going to be as big. Revel in Hobart's 'boutique' scale at this atmospheric city pub (p50), with open fires, excellent beers and plenty of quiet corners in which to pursue the lost art of conversation.

❸ Hope & Anchor

If the Brunswick is Australia's second-oldest pub, the Hope & Anchor (p51) is the oldest! Licenced since 1807, if the walls here could talk it'd be a helluva loud conversation. The upstairs dining room is festooned with amazing historical knickknacks.

❹ Telegraph Hotel

Down on the waterfront, act like a longshoreman and mosey into this old art-deco pub (Map p68, B5; ☎03-6234 6254; www.facebook. com/telegraphhotel; 19 Morrison St, Hobart; ⏰11am-late). Despite being afflicted by an infectious rash of 1990s turquoise tiles and corrugated iron, 'the Telly' still has boat-loads of charm.

❺ Customs House Hotel

Across the road from Parliament House, the sandstone Customs House Hotel (p65) is in a prime waterfront position. Resisting the urge to hipster-fy itself, it's a determinedly old-school spot for a beer.

❻ The Whaler

Formerly the much-adored Knopwoods Retreat, The Whaler (p80) is doing its best not to annoy anyone who might consider venturing back here after the name change. Uncomplicated and open-to-all-comers, it's something of an anomaly on slick Salamanca Place.

❼ Shipwright's Arms Hotel

When the Sydney to Hobart Yacht Race fleet sweeps into Hobart just prior to New Year's Eve, most of the yachties end up at 'Shippies (p124)' – a classic backstreet Battery Point boozer that's been here since 1846. Whose shout?

Battery Point, Sandy Bay & South Hobart

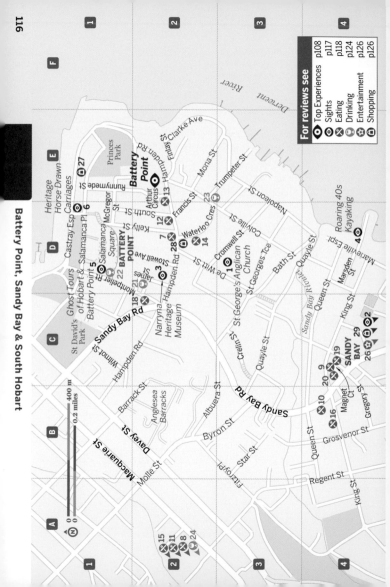

Dervent River

Battery Point

Heritage Horse Drawn Carriages

St David's Park

Ghost Tours of Hobart

Sandy Bay Rd

SANDY BAY

Anglesea Barracks

Davey St

Macquaire St

Molle St

0   400 m
0   0.2 miles

Sights

St George's Anglican Church

CHURCH

1 👁 MAP P116, D3

Designed by colonial architect John Lee Archer (with a tower designed by convict James Blackburn), this landmark 1838 church sits atop the highest bit of land in Battery Point. It's visible from all over southern Hobart, and from out on the river (returning sailors would use it as a beacon).

A small church museum is open by appointment. (📞03-6223 2146; www.stgeorgesbatterypoint.org; 30 Cromwell St, Battery Point; 🕑office 9.15am-2.15pm Mon-Thu, services 8am & 10am Sun)

Lower Sandy Bay Beach

BEACH

2 👁 MAP P116, C4

This sweet little beach is a decent spot for a stroll or a dip on a hot afternoon: swim out to the pontoon and warm up in the sun before re-entering the chilly brine. The Hobart Twilight Market (p127) happens nearby. (Long Beach; Beach Rd, Lower Sandy Bay)

Narryna Heritage Museum

MUSEUM

3 👁 MAP P116, D2

Fronted by a babbling fountain, this stately Greek-Revival sandstone mansion (pronounced 'Narrina') was built in 1837 by trader Captain Andrew Haig.

St George's Anglican Church

SHERWINATOR/SHUTTERSTOCK ©

Battery Point, Sandy Bay & South Hobart Sights

World Heritage South Hobart

In 2010 Unesco inscribed 11 Australian convict sites onto its register of places of 'outstanding universal value'. Tasmania contains five of these sites, including South Hobart's Cascades Female Factory Historic Site (p132), off Cascade Rd, where female convicts (25% of transportees) were imprisoned and put to work in miserable conditions.

Set in established grounds, it's a treasure trove of domestic colonial artefacts, and is Australia's oldest folk museum. (03-6234 2791; www.tmag.tas.gov.au/narryna; 103 Hampden Rd, Battery Point; adult/child $10/4; 10am-5pm Tue-Sat)

Roaring 40s Kayaking

KAYAKING

4 MAP P116, D4

Hobart looks its prettiest from the water. Take a safe, steady, 2½-hour guided paddle with Roaring 40s, named after the prevailing winds at these latitudes. You'll cruise from Sandy Bay, rounding Battery Point and heading into Constitution Dock for some fish and chips while you float, before returning to Sandy Bay. (0455 949 777; www.roaring40skayaking. com.au; Marieville Esplanade, Sandy Bay; adult/child $90/60; 10am Oct-Apr, 10am & 4pm Nov-Mar)

Ghost Tours of Hobart & Battery Point

WALKING

5 MAP P116, D1

Walking tours of Battery Point oozing ectoplasmic tall tales, departing the 7D Cinema on Montpelier Retreat at dusk most nights. Bookings essential, and no kids under eight. At the time of writing its city-centre tour was being reinvented. (0467 687 004; www.ghosttoursofhobart.com.au; adult/child $25/15)

Heritage Horse Drawn Carriages

TOURS

6 MAP P116, D1

Clamber into an old-fashioned horse-drawn buggy and clip-clop around the waterfront, Salamanca Place and Battery Point. It's all a bit twee, but what gorgeous animals! Tours run from 15 to 90 minutes. (0408 763 392; www.hobarthorsetours.com.au; 1 Castray Esp, Hobart; tours $60-200; tours daily)

Eating

Jackman & McRoss

BAKERY $

7 MAP P116, D2

Make sure you stop by this enduring Hobart favourite, even if it's just to gawk at the display cabinet full of delectable pies, tarts, baguettes and pastries. Breakfasts involve scrambled egg, bacon and avocado panini or potato, asparagus and brie frittatas, or perhaps just grab

Heritage Horse Drawn Carriages

a duck, cranberry and walnut sausage roll.

There's also a **branch** (☎03-6231 0601; 4 Victoria St; items $4-14, breakfast $6-15; ⏲7am-4.30pm Mon-Fri) in the city. (☎03-6223 3186; 57-59 Hampden Rd, Battery Point; items $4-14, breakfast $6-15; ⏲7am-5pm)

Ginger Brown
CAFE $

8 MAP P116, A2

This perennially popular and well-run cafe presents a wide-ranging menu, including a house crumpet with raspberry mascarpone and lemon curd, a black quinoa salad and a poke bowl. It's very kid- and cyclist-friendly, and the coffee is the best in South Hobart. Last orders 3pm. Grab the window bench for fine views of kunanyi/Mt Wellington. (☎03-6223 3531; 464 Macquarie St, South Hobart; mains $10-20; ⏲7.30am-4pm Mon-Fri, from 8.30am Sat & Sun;)

Liv-eat
CAFE $

9 MAP P116, C4

Soups, grilled salads, rolls, sandwiches, wraps, juices and smoothies – all of it fresh and/or made on the spot, and none of it deep-fried. It's a healthy formula not necessarily in accord with the lifestyles of the beer-soaked students who seem to flock here. It might be the good coffee they're after... Check the website for other branches around town. (☎03-6224 1999; www.liveat.com.au; 15 Magnet Ct, Sandy Bay; mains $7-14; ⏲6am-8.30pm;)

Sash Coffee

CAFE **$**

10 MAP P116, B4

This urbane little caffeine crevice in the main bank of Sandy Bay shops has a few stools out the front and awesome plates of brioche French toast with banana, lemon curd and vanilla ice cream. The house fruit-and-nut loaf is fab, too. Oh, and kickin' coffee! (📞0449 799 664; www.facebook.com/sashcoffee; 1/163 Sandy Bay Rd, Sandy Bay; mains $8-12; 🕐6am-5.30pm Mon-Fri, 7am-5pm Sat & Sun)

Macquarie St Foodstore

CAFE **$**

11 MAP P116, A2

It's a little way out of the city, but an excursion to the Foodstore – a pioneering South Hobart cafe –

always rewards. It's an old shop front full of booths, bookish students, brunching friends, and kids mooching around under the tables. Reconstitute over a halloumi and beetroot salad after a visit to the Cascade Brewery. (📞03-6224 6862; www.facebook.com/356foodstore; 356 Macquarie St, South Hobart; mains $9-18; 🕐7.30am-5pm Mon-Fri, 8am-5pm Sat & Sun)

Ristorante Da Angelo

ITALIAN **$$**

12 MAP P116, D2

An enduring (and endearing) Italian *ristorante*, Da Angelo presents an impressively long menu of homemade pastas, veal and chicken dishes, calzones, and pizzas with 20 different toppings. Colosseum images and Carlton

Jackman & McRoss (p118)

MARTIN BERRY/ALAMY STOCK PHOTO ©

Football Club team photos add a unique authenticity. Takeaway, BYO and open late. (☎03-6223 7011; www.daangelo.com; 47 Hampden Rd, Battery Point; mains $17-38; ☺5pm-late)

Magic Curries INDIAN $$

13 ✗ MAP P116, E2

There's a photo on the wall here of the Indian cricket team's visit in 2004 – a while ago, we know, but if it's good enough for Anil Kumble, it's good enough for us. Sip a Kingfisher beer in the magically coloured interior and await your face-meltingly hot beef vindaloo. Excellent vegetarian options; takeaway available. (☎03-6223 4500; www.magiccurries.com.au; 41 Hampden Rd, Battery Point; mains $14-22; ☺5-9.30pm Sun-Thu, to 10pm Fri & Sat; ✐)

Three Japanese JAPANESE $$

14 ✗ MAP P116, D2

Run by (you guessed it) three Japanese friends, this mod little black-and-white restaurant sources its produce as much as possible from organic producers around southern Tasmania: mushrooms from Cygnet, pork from the Huon Valley, vegetables from Bagdad. Try the Wagyu rice bowl, and scan the collection of soy and sake bottles at the front counter on your way out. (☎03-6224 1606; www.threejapanese.com.au; 38 Waterloo Cres, Battery Point; mains $18-26; ☺5-9pm Wed & Thu, 5-10pm Sat & Sun)

Battery Point Access �a

Oddly, Battery Point can seem a bit difficult to access from Salamanca Place and the waterfront – there's a huge cliff in the way! (Salamanca Square was once a quarry). To get there via a sneaky shortcut, duck down a little alleyway at the eastern end of Salamanca Place and dogleg up Kelly's Steps (signposted), a sandstone stairway built in 1839 to navigate the precipice.

Vanidol's ASIAN $$

15 ✗ MAP P116, A2

Vanidol's in North Hobart proved to be such a winner that Vanidol's in South Hobart was spawned. It's a marginally less atmospheric set-up than in 'NoHo', but the food is just as awesome. Try the Nepalese lamb curry. (☎03-6224 5986; www.vanidolsouth.com; 361a Macquarie St, South Hobart; lunch mains $15-22, dinner $22-31; ☺11am-2pm & 5.30-9pm Tue-Sat)

Solo Pasta & Pizza ITALIAN $$

16 ✗ MAP P116, B4

The brilliant pastas, pizzas, risottos and calzones at Solo have been drawing hungry hordes for decades. Not that you'd know its age from looking at it: the snazzy glass-fronted room backed by racks of wine is almost

Hobart Gothic

Hobart is a uniquely fated town, crossed with a gothic, otherworldly spirit that seems to hang in the cobweb corners of the latitude. People have suffered here – indigenous Tasmanians and convicts – a grim legacy that can't be rewound or dismissed.

The Mountain & the Muwinina

Rising behind South Hobart is kunanyi/Mt Wellington (p136) – *kunanyi* is the mountain's indigenous Muwinina name – its broad dolerite mass brooding and omnipresent in the icy wind. Beneath the mountain, a profound sense of loss and oblivion can bear down, and with it the thought that western civilisation should never have arrived.

Indeed, before the British arrived in 1803, the Muwinina lived here harmoniously for tens of thousands of years, maintaining a stable seasonal culture of hunting, fishing and gathering. In the early 1800s they watched from Kunanyi as the intruders cleared trees and built their city below. It's reasonable to consider that the first bloom of British sail cloth on the Derwent – and with it the guns, disease and alcohol that decimated Tasmania's Aboriginal population – has somehow cursed this place.

Convicted

Then came the convicts. Around 70,000 British criminals were sent to Tasmania up until the 1850s and locked in prisons so inhumane that today, among their ruins, the sense of sadness is palpable. The Port Arthur Historic Site southeast of Hobart is the prime example: even on sunny days the vibe here is grim (not helped by memories of the 1996 massacre here, when a lone gunman killed 35 people).

Back in South Hobart, the Cascades Female Factory Historic Site (p132) was where female convicts were incarcerated and made to work in vile conditions. Children suffered here, too: convict women sent to work on settler's farms would often return pregnant, give birth to their illegitimate children, then try desperately to keep them alive. It's said that when the Hobart Rivulet floods at the end of Degraves St, the bones of children sometimes wash loose among the dirt.

futuristic. (📞03-6234 9898; www.solopastaandpizza.com.au; 50b King St, Sandy Bay; mains $16-34; ⏱5-10pm Tue-Sun)

Signal Station Brasserie
MODERN AUSTRALIAN $$

17 ✕ MAP P116

Lunch with a view? Grab a window table at this elegant, glass-fronted brasserie with awesome Derwent River views, inside Mt Nelson's 120-year-old signalman's house. Try the salmon cured in beetroot, vodka and gin with smashed potatoes and pickled cucumber-and-radish salad. (📞03-6223 3407; www.signalstation.com.au; 700 Nelson Rd, Mt Nelson; breakfast mains $13-23, lunch $24-32; ⏱10am-4pm Mon-Fri, 9am-4pm Sat & Sun)

Hearth
PIZZA $$

18 ✕ MAP P116, C2

Pull up a table by the blackened hearth at, ah, Hearth, a lovely old brick house just off Sandy Bay Rd, serving small plates to share or interesting pizzas to selfishly devour. Try the pulled-lamb-shoulder pizza with red-onion marmalade and feta. Takeaways available. (📞03-6223 2511; www.hearthpizza.com.au; 37 Montpelier Retreat, Battery Point; small plates $9-22, pizzas $20-36; ⏱5-9pm Sun-Thu, to 10pm Fri & Sat)

Me Wah
CHINESE $$$

19 ✕ MAP P116, C4

From the outside, Me Wah looks just like any suburban shopping-mall joint. But inside it's an elegant confection of chinoiserie, almost bordering on over-the-top. The food is equally stellar, including terrific ways with seafood and world-famous-in-Hobart yum cha sessions from 11am on weekends. Plenty of vegetarian choices. (📞03-6223 3688; www.mewah.com.au; 16 Magnet Ct, Sandy Bay; mains $19-42, banquets per person from $65; ⏱noon-2.30pm & 6-9.30pm Tue-Sun; 🍴)

Don Camillo
ITALIAN $$$

20 ✕ MAP P116, C4

Claiming to be Hobart's oldest restaurant (since 1965), venerable Don Camillo is still turning out a tight menu of classic Italian pastas, risottos, meat dishes and Mama's cassata – no pizzas here – on red-checked tablecloths. Look for the red Vespa parked out the front. (📞03-6234 1006; www.doncamillorestaurant.com; 5 Magnet Ct, Sandy Bay; mains $28-42; ⏱11.30am-2.30pm Thu & Fri, 5.30-9.30pm Tue-Sat)

In Like Flynn

Legendary swashbuckling actor Errol Flynn was born in Battery Point, first showing his handsome, future-moustachioed face at the Queen Alexandra Hospital on Hampden Rd on 20 June 1909. Flynn lived in Hobart, where his father was a professor of biology, until he was sent to school in London at the rather pivotal age of 14. Flynn went on to become a swashbuckling Hollywood superstar – lighting up the screen in films like *Captain Blood* and *The Adventures of Robin Hood* – and a notorious ladies' man (hence the phrase 'In Like Flynn'), before expiring prematurely at age 50 whilst visiting Canada.

Drinking

Preachers   BAR

21 🚇 MAP P116, D2

Hipster beards are optional but preferred at this 1849 sailmaker's cottage turned bar. The ramshackle beer garden is the place to be in Hobart on a summer evening, while the retro sofa inside is a warm hibernation den in winter. Great list of craft beers and wine, while the burgers keep the inebriation in vague check. (📞03-6223 3621; www.facebook.com/preachershobart; 5 Knopwood St, Battery Point; ⏱noon-11.30pm)

Society Salamanca   COCKTAIL BAR

22 🚇 MAP P116, D1

Society Salamanca is an atmospheric gin-and-whisky bar occupying the ground floor of a brutal-looking concrete building just up the hill from Salamanca Place. Try some Brocken Spectre gin, distilled a few hundred metres away in Battery Point. Tapas on Tuesday from 6pm. (📞03-6223 1497; http://societysalamanca.com; 22 Montpellier Retreat, Hobart; ⏱4pm-late Tue-Sat)

Shipwrights Arms Hotel   PUB

23 🚇 MAP P116, E2

Traditionally the first stop in town for Sydney to Hobart Yacht Race sailors, the walls of backstreet 'Shippies' are a cluttered ode to the great race. Soak yourself in maritime heritage (and other liquids) at the bar, then retire to the bistro for a hefty pub meal.

You can get a clean, above-board berth upstairs or in the newer wing (doubles with/without bathroom $150/90). (📞03-6223 1846; www.shipwrightsarms.com.au; 29 Trumpeter St, Battery Point; ⏱11.30am-late; 📶)

Cascade Hotel

PUB

24 🚇 MAP P116, A2

Almost within eyeshot of Cascade Brewery just around the corner, this old pub has been pouring the local product since 1846. These days it's a reliable locals' hangout with good food and occasional live music, including free-wheeling jazz jams every Wednesday night. (☏03-6223 6385; www.cascadehotel.com.au; 22 Cascade Rd, South Hobart; ⏲10am-9pm Mon-Thi, to 10pm Fri & Sat, to 8pm Sun)

Fern Tree Tavern

PUB

25 🚇 MAP P116

This low-lying 1960s tavern at Fern Tree, half way up Mt Wellington, really should be pumping with hungry and thirsty visitors, warming up by the open fires or cooling down with cold beers after their mountain adventures. But there's never anyone here! Enjoy the solitude. (☏03-6239 1171; www.facebook.com/ ferntreetavern; 680 Huon Rd, Fern Tree; ⏲noon-8pm Tue-Thu, to 9pm Fri, 10.30am-9pm Sat & Sun)

Shipwrights Arms Hotel

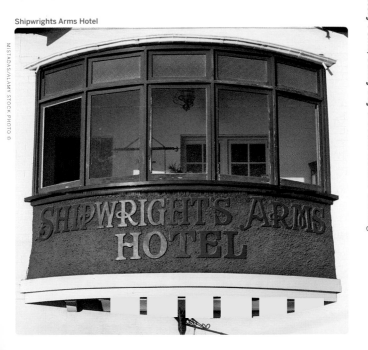

Entertainment

Wrest Point Casino

LIVE PERFORMANCE

26 ⭐ MAP P116, C4

This 17-storey octagonal tower on the Sandy Bay waterfront opened in 1973 as Australia's first casino, and has been the subject of many a postcard from Hobart ever since. Gambling is still the mainstay, but concert venues (and outdoor lawns) host big touring rock, comedy and theatre shows. (📞03-6221 1888; www.wrestpoint.com.au; 410 Sandy Bay Rd, Sandy Bay; 🕐performance times vary)

Shopping

Despard Gallery

ART

27 🔒 MAP P116, E1

This is where you will find top-notch contemporary Tasmanian arts – glassware, jewellery,

Concert at Wrest Point Casino

JOEL EVERARD/SHUTTERSTOCK ©

Whales in the Derwent

In the 1830s Hobartians joked about walking across the Derwent River on the backs of whales and complained about being kept awake at night by whales cavorting offshore. A glance across the river from from Battery Point or Sandy Bay might reveal any number of spouting blowholes and splashing flukes. Typically, the ensuing whaling boom was catastrophic for the whales, driving local populations of southern right and humpback whales to near extinction.

Though still endangered, the occasional forgiving whale returns to the Derwent during June-July northbound and October-November southbound migration. If you spy one, call the Parks & Wildlife Service whale hotline on 0427 WHALES (0427 942 537).

canvases and ceramics – in a lovely old sandstone building a short stroll from Salamanca Place. (03-6223 8266; www. despard-gallery.com.au; 15 Castray Esplanade, Battery Point; ☉10am-6pm Mon-Fri, to 4pm Sat, 11am-4pm Sun)

On Hampden Creative
GIFTS & SOUVENIRS

28 🔒 MAP P116, D2

Excellent little two-room Battery Point shop selling little handmade Tasmanian things: jewellery, candles, soaps, scarves and pots of leatherwood honey and raspberry jam. (0414 518 739; 66 Hampden Rd, Battery Point; ☉10am-5pm Mon-Fri, to 3pm Sat & Sun)

Hobart Twilight Market
MARKET

29 🔒 MAP P116, C4

Filling the lawns behind Lower Sandy Bay Beach (aka Long Beach; about 5km south of central Hobart), this summer market runs to a beat of waves and live music. The official line goes, 'eats, drinks, design, music', and you'll find hand-made clothing, crockery, jewellery, food, wine, and dog treats for the abundance of canines.

A courtesy shuttle to the market leaves from outside the waterfront office of Pennicott Wilderness Journeys (p70) at 5pm, 6pm and 7pm. (HTM; 0448 997 748; www.facebook.com/hobarttwilightmarket; 17 Beach Rd, Lower Sandy Bay; ☉4.30-9pm Fri Oct-Mar)

Worth a Trip 🔭

Tour the Cascade Brewery

Even for Aussies who don't drink beer (yes, there are a few), the name 'Cascade' is synonymous with Tasmania, and Hobart in particular. On the banks of the Hobart Rivulet in South Hobart, this is Australia's oldest brewery (1832) – and is a rather arresting piece of architecture to boot. Brewery tours have become an essential Hobart experience.

☎ 03-6212 7801

www.cascadebrewery.
com.au

140 Cascade Rd, South
Hobart

brewery tour adult/child
16-18yr $30/15, Beer
School adult/child $15/10

History & Architecture

Woah, check out that facade! It's fair to say that upon first sight, the towering Cascade building is more than a little spooky-looking, especially on a cold winter's day when there's snow on Mt Wellington and the sun doesn't reach into this wet corner of South Hobart for more than an hour or two.

From modest beginnings in 1832 when the first Cascade beer was sold (stemming from an original brewing operation set up in 1824), Cascade grew to monopolise beer sales in southern Tasmania by the 1900s. The brewery's marvellous facade dates from 1927, designed by local architects Glaskin and Ricards to build upon existing structures. The facade almost didn't make it past 1967, when devastating bushfires blazed through many Hobart suburbs and all but destroyed the brewery. But the thirsty Hobart community rallied and rebuilt Cascade: amazingly, the beloved brewery was pumping out beer again within three months.

Brewery Tour

Brewery tours leave from the visitor centre across the road from the iconic main brewery building. The main tour (what most people are here for) takes you into the factory workings to see how Cascade's beers are assembled from base ingredients: water, malt, hops and yeast. Be prepared to tackle a lot of stairs, which only serves to prime your thirst when it comes time to taste the product at tour's end. Tours last 90 minutes, departing four to seven times daily.

Note that if you're here on a weekend, some of the brewery machinery may not be running.

★ **Top Tips**

○ Tour numbers are limited: book in advance (online).

○ Tour safety rules: no booze beforehand; no loose jewellery; legs must be fully covered; only enclosed, flat shoes.

✗ **Take a Break**

One of Hobart's best cafes is nearby Ginger Brown (p119) – perfect for a quick lunch.

The Cascade Hotel (p125) is a resolutely old-school South Hobart boozer.

★ **Getting There**

Car From the city take Davey St then dogleg onto Macquarie St, which becomes Cascade Rd – a 3.5km trip

Bus 446, 447, 448 or 449 from the city centre.

All-Ages Experiences
Aside from the main brewery tour (for folks aged 16 and over), there are two other tours that the whole family can enjoy (no tastings or factory access).

Cascade Story A garden tour running for 45 minutes, looking at the history of the brewery, brewing in Hobart more generally, and highlighting some of the characters who've played a part in Cascade's evolution. Tours run once daily, four days a week during school holiday periods – usually Tuesday and Friday to Sunday.

In the Shadow Historical Play A dramatic re-enactment of the life and trials of Sophia Degraves, wife of Cascade founder Peter Degraves (was he casting a shadow over Sophia, or was it Mt Wellington?). Tours run once daily, three days a week – Monday,

Peter Degraves
Back in 1832, the Cascade Brewery's founder was one Mr Peter Degraves – a visionary and a bullish businessman, certainly, but also a bankrupt and convicted thief who served time in Hobart for his crimes. Nearby Degraves St is named after him.

Friday and Saturday – and last 45 minutes.

Summer Jazz
A further enticement at Cascade is the Summer Jazz Festival, a series of outdoor gigs, every Sunday afternoon from early December to the end of February. Kick back on a rug and sip your way into the local product to a smooth bee-bop and zah-ba-de-bah soundtrack.

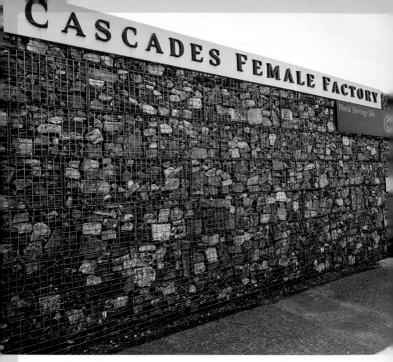

Worth a Trip 🔭

Witness History at Cascades Female Factory Historic Site

For more than a century most Hobartians lived in blissful ignorance about this storied South Hobart convict site, reduced as it was to crumbling walls, weed-filled yards and sundry outbuildings purloined into other uses. Recently listed by Unesco as a site of major historic significance, this former female prison is now high on the 'must-see' list of many visitors to Hobart.

📱 03-6233 6656, 1800 139 478

www.femalefactory.org.au

16 Degraves St, South Hobart

adult/child/family $8/5/20, Heritage Tour $18/12/45

Tasmania's Female Convicts

It's a rather staggering fact that one in four convicts sent to Van Diemen's Land from Britain – around 12,500 between 1803 and 1853 – was female. So grim was life in the UK for unmarried, uneducated, impoverished young women that many of these transportees committed deliberate crimes in order to be sent to the other side of the planet, hoping that their lives would somehow improve – could they be any worse? Unfortunately, for many who ended up at the Female Factory in South Hobart, which opened in 1828 on the site of a failed distillery, the answer was 'yes'.

Convict Life for Women

The Female Factory wasn't just a prison, it was also a work house and a processing plant for sending women out into the colony as (essentially) slave labour for affluent settlers.

Classified into three groups based on the seriousness of their misdemeanours, women were put to work cooking, sewing, laundering and spinning wool for up to 12 hours a day, often in freezing, wet conditions. Any insubordination was punishable by close, solitary confinement in darkened cells. Sleeping conditions were cramped, often with 600 women crammed into a facility designed for 200.

Those sent out to work in the colony faced a different menace. Land and estate owners often saw the provision of sexual favours as part of the contract between them and their servants. Many women, unable to conceal their resultant pregnancies for very long, would be returned to the Female Factory and labelled as shameful sinners. Many illegitimate children were born here, with many of them succumbing to the cold, wet, louse-ridden living conditions.

★ Top Tips

○ Beat the crowds: get in early for the 10am Heritage Tour.

○ You can visit the site without taking a tour, but the Heritage Tour ($10) and 'Her Story' re-enactment ($20) really help with interpretation.

✗ Take a Break

For a pan-Asian lunch or dinner, swing into the excellent Vanidol's (p121).

★ Getting There

Car Degraves St in South Hobart is the extension of McRobies Rd, which is, itself, off Macquarie St.

Bus 446, 447, 448 or 449 from the city centre

★ Opening Times

○ General opening hours are 9.30am-4pm,

○ Tours take place at 10am, 11am, 1pm, 2pm & 3pm

Interpreting the Past

When convict transportation to Van Diemen's Land ceased in 1853, the Female Factory was slowly wound down, eventually closing in 1877. It's a measure of how much shame Tasmanians have heaped on their convict past that so little of the Female Factory's original built fabric remains. Much of the complex was demolished, carted away, sold off and built over, or just left to crumble. You can enter the site and look around without taking a tour, but as the remains are so scant, a tour is the best way of interpreting what you see.

Tours & Experiences

Forty-five-minute guided **Heritage Tours** run seven days a week at 10am, 11am, 1pm, 2pm and 3pm, regardless of what the weather sees fit to provide (on a wet winter morning the

On the Town

A common misconception about female convicts transported to Van Diemen's Land is that they were mostly prostitutes being punished for their profession. Convict ship records would label a prisoner as 'on the town' if indeed they had been a prostitute, but this term was also applied to vagrant transportees who'd been living on church benefaction. Percentages of convicts listed as 'on the town' generally ranged between 20% and 40%.

atmosphere here is palpably grim). Guides shed light on the site's remaining and demolished built structures, and give some insights into punishment, work and reform at the 'factory'.

Worth a Trip 👀
Climb kunanyi/Mt Wellington

Known as kunanyi to the local Muwinina Aboriginal people, 1271m-high Mt Wellington is a serious chunk of stone. Dolerite, in fact, violently intruded between layers of older rock when Australia ripped itself away from Antarctica around 40 million years ago. These days kunanyi is Hobart's beacon, its protector and its barometer...and the views from the top are awesome!

www.wellingtonpark.org.au

Pinnacle Rd, via Fern Tree

The Summit

The sealed 12km Pinnacle Rd from Fern Tree to the Mt Wellington summit was the brainchild of Albert Ogilvie, premier of Tasmania in the 1930s. When the Great Depression hit hard in Hobart, Ogilvie deemed that all those unemployed hands would be best engaged in doing something constructive for the community. After several years of backbreaking labour, Pinnacle Rd opened in 1937. Initially very visible from the city and not entirely popular, the road became know as 'Ogilvie's Scar'.

These days the road has mostly been obscured by trees; much more visible are the two huge transmission towers at the peak. There's a nifty little curvy-roofed viewing room here, too, in which you can shelter from the wind and check out the eye-popping views. A drive to the summit to assess the city below is now a near-mandatory Hobart experience. Don't be deterred if the sky looks overcast from sea level: often the summit rises above the gloom, and the view from the top extends across a magical sea of rolling white cloud-tops.

Hiking & Biking

The mountain is criss-crossed by numerous hiking paths, bike tracks, horse-riding trails and fire roads, some well-trodden and wide, some overgrown and intriguing. Popular tracks include the Radfords Track, Pinnacle Track, Fern Glade Track, the steep Zig Zag Track and the Organ Pipes track below kunanyi's trademark cliffs. Check out www. greaterhobarttrails.com.au for detailed track and planning info. At any time on the mountain, expect rapid and extreme weather shifts: this ain't no walk in the park (well, it is, but you know what we mean – be prepared).

For an excellent mountain-bike experience, tackle the **Mt Wellington Descent** (✐1800

★ **Top Tips**

o The fabulous www. wellingtonpark.org. au is a wealth of maps, history and bushwalking and mountain-biking info.

o Mt Wellington's weather is notoriously fickle: be ready for snow and 100km/h winds in December and warm sunshine and twittering birds in June.

o For Pinnacle Rd snow-closure updates see www. hobartcity.com.au.

✕ **Take a Break**

At forested Fern Tree, halfway up the hill, the rudimentary Fern Tree Tavern (p125) has cold beer and warm fires.

★ **Getting There**

Car Take Davey St from the city centre to Fern Tree, then Pinnacle Rd to the summit (19km).

Bus 448 (direct) or 447 or 449 (indirect) to Fern Tree.

444 442; www.underdownunder.com.au/tour/mount-wellington-descent; adult/child $85/65; ⏱10am & 1pm year-round, plus 4pm Dec-Feb). Take a van ride to the summit, then enjoy 22km of super-scenic downhill cruising (mostly – the last 5km are flat) on a mountain bike. It's terrific fun, with minimal energy output and maximum views! Tours start and end at 4 Elizabeth St on the Hobart waterfront (near the visitor information centre), and last 2½ hours.

Winter Snow

Sure, Canberra has sub-zero nights and Melbourne requires one to don a woolly hat occasionally, but do any Australian cities other than Hobart have access to ACTUAL SNOW!? 'No', is the resounding response. Mt Wellington wears a white cloak for most of the winter (June to August), with snowfalls often reaching down into the suburbs. Local kids grow up knowing what it's like to build a snowman, hurl a snowball and pile a snow mound on the car bonnet for the ride back to sea level, watching in anticipation for the moment it melts and slides off onto the road.

Lost World

A real local secret (not so secret now, eh?), Lost World is an amazing boulder field near the peak of Mt Wellington, backed by a miniature version of the famous Organ Pipes dolerite cliffs below

The Springs

About half way up Pinnacle Rd is a place called the Springs, where once stood a popular hotel and health spa. The verandah-wrapped 'Hotel Mount Wellington' opened in 1907 – a lavish, two-storey Victorian timber chalet, with 16 guest rooms, hot and cold running water, and drawing, sitting, dining and smoking rooms. Sadly the hotel, like many other buildings and huts on the mountain's lower flanks, was destroyed by Hobart's devastating 1967 bushfires. These days, **Bentwood Coffee** (☎0417 719 856; www.lostfreightcafe.com; items $5-8; ⏱9am-4pm Mon-Fri, 8.30am-5pm Sat & Sun, shorter hours in winter) fills the Springs' hospitality niche – a cool little caravan warming up passing mountaineers.

the summit, further to the south. Rock climbers, boulder-hoppers and bushwalkers venture here to lose a few hours in surreal solitude, to check out the views, or to play hide-and-seek among the massive fractured hunks of stone.

To get to Lost World, take the little track heading north from the car park at 'Big Bend', 9km up Pinnacle Rd from Fern Tree – the last major hairpin bend before the summit. It's a 45-minute walk one-way.

Survival Guide

Victoria Dock (p65) CYRUS_2000/SHUTTERSTOCK ©

Before You Go

Book Your Stay

○ Hobart has plenty of budget hostels and pubs offering accommodation, some salubrious, some not so much...

○ Like the rest of Tasmania, midrange accommodation here isn't exactly a bargain (B&Bs and motels, mostly).

○ Conversely, top-end accommodation can be quite reasonable. If your budget stretches beyond $250 per night, you can afford something quite special: designer hotels, historic guesthouses and mod waterside apartments.

○ Booking ahead is always a good idea, regardless of season.

Useful Websites

Discover Tasmania (www.discover tasmania.com.au) Comprehensive listings in Hobart and across the state.

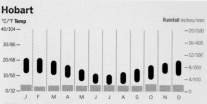

When to Go

Summer (Dec–Feb)
Peak tourist season: the weather is at its warmest and big-ticket events keep the hordes entertained.

Autumn (Mar–May)
Atmospheric autumn leaves and smoky evenings. Easter is busy (late March or early April) – book beds ahead.

Winter (Jun–Aug)
It's cold, but there's snow on kunanyi/Mt Wellington and the Dark MOFO festival warms Hobart's collective soul.

Spring (Sep–Nov)
Spring brings flower blooms and optimism – and it's the perfect time to sidestep the crowds.

Hobart & Beyond (www.hobartand beyond.com) Select Hobart listings.

Lonely Planet (www. lonelyplanet.com/ australia/tasmania/ hobart/hotels) Recommendations and bookings.

Best Budget

Montacute (www. montacute.com.au) Assess the aesthetics of the other flash-packers in Hobart's best hostel.

The Nook (www.the nookbackpackers.com. au) Hobart's newest hostel-in-a-converted-pub makes a good job of it.

Alabama Hotel (www. alabamahobart.com. au) Fab retro pub conversion in the city centre.

Tassie Backpackers (www.brunswick hotelhobart.com. au) Upstairs at the venerable old Brunswick Hotel is one of Hobart's better hostels.

Hobart Central YHA

(www.yha.com.au) A predictably clean, tidy and well-managed city YHA.

Hobart's Accommodation & Hostel

(www.hobarthostel. com) Above-board backpackers in a converted pub on the city fringe.

Best Midrange

Astor Private Hotel

(www.astorprivate-hotel.com.au) Endearing old hotel in the city with boundless charm.

Quayle Terrace (www. quayleterrace.com. au) Renovated Battery Point terrace house, perfect for a small family.

Old Woolstore Apartment Hotel

(www.oldwoolstore. com.au) Play international CEO at these slick waterside apartments.

Apartments on Star

(www.apartments onstar.com.au) Nifty contemporary apartments in an excellent Sandy bay location.

Quest Savoy (www. questapartments. com.au) Super-duper

modern studios in a converted downtown bank.

Altamont House

(www.airbnb.com.au/ rooms/5353814) A plush double suite in a gorgeous 1854 stone-and-slate house in West Hobart.

Best Top End

Grande Vue Private Hotel (www.grande-

vue-hotel.com) The best B&B in the city has gorgeous river and mountain views.

Islington (www. islingtonhotel.com) Opulent homestead in atmospheric South Hobart.

Henry Jones Art Hotel

(www.thehenryjones. com) Boutique waterside warehouse conversion hung with gorgeous art.

Somerset on the

Pier (www.somerset. oom) You want water views with that? Fab apartments in Elizabeth St Pier.

Salamanca Wharf

Hotel (www.salamanca wharfhotel.com) Slick new one-bedroom apartments just east of Salamanca Place.

Sullivans Cove Apartments (www.

sullivanscove apartments.com. au) Sassy boutique apartments, dotted around the Hobart waterfront in five locations.

Arriving in Hobart

Hobart Airport

In an irony that doesn't elude the locals, Hobart's 'international' **airport** (☏ 03-6216 1600; www. hobartairport.com.au; 6 Hinkler Rd, Cambridge) has only domestic flights (perhaps we should commend the optimism?). The airport is at Cambridge, 19km east of the city.

○ Services are operated by **Qantas** (☏ 13 13 13; www.qantas.com.au), **Virgin Australia** (☏ 13 67 89; www.virginaustralia. com) and **Jetstar** (☏ 13 15 38; www.jetstar.com. au), with direct flights from Melbourne, Sydney, Brisbane and sometimes Canberra.

o There's no public transport to Hobart Airport.

o Many visitors to Hobart rent a car: rental desks proliferate in the airport terminal.

o A taxi into the city will cost around $50 and take about 20 minutes.

o Pre-booked Hobart Airporter shuttle buses meet every flight and can deliver you door-to-door.

Devonport Ferry Terminal

If you're arriving by ferry from Melbourne aboard the **Spirit of Tasmania** (☏03-6419 9320, 1800 634 906; www.spiritoftasmania. com.au; 🛜), the big red boat spits you out in Devonport on Tasmania's northwest coast. It's a 3¼-hour drive from here to Hobart.

Bus Stations

The main intrastate bus company operating here is **Redline Coaches** (☏1300 360 000; www. tasredline.com.au; 230 Liverpool St; 🕑9am-1.15pm & 2.15-6pm Mon-Fri,

9am-noon & 12.30-3.30pm Sat, 9am-noon, 1-4pm & 4.30-6pm Sun).

o Redline buses arrive/ depart from their office at 230 Liverpool St.

o Check online for fares, routes and timetables.

Main Access Roads

o From the airport, east coast or Tasman Peninsula, the approach to the city is via the Tasman Bridge (A3).

o From the north (eg from the car ferry), the view of the city from the high-point of the Brooker Hwy (Hwy 1) will give you a good sense of the lay of the land.

o From the south, the approach is via the steep Southern Outlet (A6) road which spits you out in South Hobart.

Getting Around

Bicycle

There are a number of bike-hire outlets around the city: it's a handy, affordable

option if the weather is looking good and you don't mind sweating it out on a hill or three.

Bus

The local bus network is operated by **Metro Tasmania** (☏13 22 01; www.metrotas.com.au), which is reliable but infrequent outside of business hours.

o The **Metro Shop** (☏13 22 01; www.metrotas.com. au; 22 Elizabeth St; 🕑8am-5.30pm Mon-Fri) handles ticketing and enquiries: most buses depart from this section of Elizabeth St, or from nearby Franklin Sq.

o One-way cash ticket prices vary with the number of zones travelled: one zone $3.30, two zones $4.60, or all zones $6.90. Fares into non-urban zones are additional to these costs.

o Buy a rechargeable **Greencard** in store or online from the Metro Shop for a 20% discount on regular fares.

o One-way tickets can be bought from the Metro Shop, the driver (exact change required), or ticket agents (news-agents and post offices).

Car & Motorcycle

This is the best way to explore Hobart. There are no toll roads here, but the CBD's one-way system can be a bit mind-boggling.

Rental

The big-boy rental firms have airport desks and city offices. Cheaper local firms offer daily rental rates from as low as $30. Note that some companies don't allow you to take their cars onto Bruny Island: ask when you book.

Parking

Timed, metered parking predominates in the CBD and tourist areas such as Salamanca Place and the waterfront. Parking inspectors here have a sixth sense – don't even think about over-staying! For longer-term parking, large CBD car parks (clearly signposted) offer reasonable rates.

Taxi

Hobart's taxi services pick up the slack from the bus network, with ranks in key areas such as Salamanca Place, North Hobart and the CBD. Or you can book one over the phone or online.

131008 Hobart (⏱ 13 10 08; www.131008hobart. com) Standard taxis.

13cabs (⏱ 13 22 27; www.13cabs.com.au) Standard cabs (some of which are yellow).

Uber (www.uber. com) also operates in Hobart.

Walking

○ Downtown Hobart is a compact area: if you're only here for a short time and aren't exploring beyond the CBD, Battery Point and waterfront, walking is a fine option.

○ If your accommodation is in West Hobart, North Hobart, Sandy Bay or beyond, you may find yourself in for a long trudge back to your bed. Do some planning before you decide to rely solely on the soles of your feet to get around.

Essential Information

Accessible Travel

○ In Hobart, an increasing number of accommodation providers and key attractions have access for those with limited mobility, and tour operators often have the appropriate facilities: call ahead to confirm.

○ Download Lonely Planet's free Accessible Travel guide from http://lptravel.to/ AccessibleTravel.

○ Also check out the *Hobart CBD Mobility Map* from the Hobart Visitor Information Centre.

Business Hours

Banks 9.30am–4pm Monday to Thursday, to 5pm Friday

Cafes 7.30am–4pm

Post Offices 9am–5pm Monday to Friday; some open Saturday morning

Pubs & Bars 11am–11pm daily (bars often close later)

Restaurants lunch noon–2pm and dinner 6pm–8.30pm

Shops 9am–5pm Monday to Friday, 9am–noon or 5pm Saturday, late-night city shopping to 8pm Friday

Electricity

Type I
230V/50Hz

Emergency

o Dial 000 for police, fire and ambulance emergencies.

o **Hobart Police Station** (☏03-6230 2111, nonemergency assistance 13 14 44; www.police.tas. gov.au; 37-43 Liverpool St; ⊙24hr) is Hobart's main cop shop.

Insurance

o A good travel insurance policy covering theft, loss and medical problems is essential.

o Some policies specifically exclude designated 'dangerous activities' such as scuba diving, surfing and even bushwalking: ensure the policy you choose fully covers you for your activity of choice, and covers ambulances and emergency medical evacuations by air.

o Worldwide travel insurance is available at www.lonelyplanet. com/travel-insurance. You can buy, extend and claim online any time – even if you're already on the road.

Internet Access

o Wireless access is fast becoming a given in most Hobart accommodation. If access is not totally free, you might still get a certain amount of data gratis, then pay-per-use after that.

o See www.freewifi. tas.gov.au for free government-sponsored wi-fi locations around the city.

o Hobart cafes and pubs have been slow to adopt free wi-fi for customers, though you can find it (you might have to ask).

o The **State Library of Tasmania** (☏03-6165 5597; http://libraries. tas.gov.au; 91 Murray St; ⊙9.30am-6pm Mon-Thu, to 7pm Fri, to 2pm Sat) has free pre-booked internet terminals.

LGBTIQ+ Travellers

It wasn't always the case, but Tasmania is now considered by LGBTIQ rights groups to have greater equality in criminal law for homosexual and heterosexual people than most other Australian states. But beyond the law, a lack of discrimination outside of urban centres should never be assumed.

Gay Tasmania (www. gaytasmania.com.au) Accommodation and travel info.

TasPride (www.tas pride.com) Info on upcoming events, including November's annual TasPride Festival.

Travel Gay (www. travelgay.com/gay-tasmania) State-wide travel info and suggestions.

Money-Saving Tips

o Central Hobart and the waterfront area are compact enough to walk around: save on taxi fares and hoof it instead.

o If you're planning on catching a lot of buses, buy a **Greencard** from **Metro Tasmania** (☑13 22 01; www.metrotas.com.au) for 20% off regular fares.

Media

Warp (www.warpmagazine. com.au) Tasmania's free music and arts street press, covering the whole state.

The Mercury (www.the mercury.com.au) Local newspaper, covering Hobart and the south.

Tasmania 40° South (www.fortysouth.com.au) An excellent quarterly magazine with food, travel and wildlife stories.

Mobile Phones

o European phones will work on Australia's network, but most American or Japanese phones will not.

o Use global roaming or buy a local SIM card with a prepaid account you can top-up.

o Local numbers with the prefix 04 belong to mobile phones.

o Reception is good throughout Hobart CBD and suburbs.

Money

The major banks all have branches and ATMs around the Elizabeth St Mall. There are also ATMs around Salamanca Place.

ATMs Hobart is flush with ATMs, from the airport to the city centre and suburban shopping strips. You'll also sometimes find a multicard ATM in the local grocery store, pub or petrol station.

Credit Cards Credit cards such as MasterCard and Visa are widely accepted for most accommodation and services, and a credit card is essential to hire a car. Diners Club and American Express cards are not as widely accepted.

Currency The Australian dollar (AUD) comprises 100 cents. There are 5c, 10c, 20c, 50c, $1 and $2 coins, and $5, $10, $20, $50 and $100 notes.

Debit Cards For international travellers, debit cards connected to the international banking networks – Cirrus, Maestro, Plus and Eurocard – will work fine in Hobart ATMs. Expect substantial fees.

A better option may be prepaid debit cards (such as MasterCard and Travelex 'Cash Passport' cards) with set withdrawal fees and a balance you can top up from your bank account while on the road.

Eftpos Almost all retail outlets have Eftpos, which allows you to pay for purchases electronically by card without a fee.

Tipping Common in Australia in many situations, but certainly not mandatory. In restaurants and upmarket cafes, tip 10% of the bill if the service warrants it.

Taxes & Refunds

o Australia has a flat 10% tax on all goods and services (GST), included in quoted/shelf prices.

o A refund is sometimes possible under the Tourist Refund Scheme (TRS); see www.border. gov.au/trav/ente/tour/ are-you-a-traveller.

Public Holidays

Hobartians observe the following public holidays:

New Year's Day
1 January

Australia Day
26 January

Hobart Regatta Day 2nd Monday in February

Eight Hour Day 2nd Monday in March

Easter March/April (Good Friday to Easter Tuesday inclusive)

Anzac Day 25 April

Queen's Birthday 2nd Monday in June

Hobart Show 3rd Thursday in October

Christmas Day
25 December

Boxing Day
26 December

School Holidays

o The Christmas/ summer school-holiday season runs from mid-December to late January.

o Three shorter school holiday periods occur during the year: roughly from early to mid-April, late June to mid-July, and late September to early October.

Responsible Travel

For tips on responsible travel around Hobart and beyond, see:
o www.tasmania.com/ things-to-do/eco-conservation

o www.responsible travel.com/holidays/ tasmania/travel-guide/ responsible-tourism-in-tasmania

o www.greataustralian secret.com/what-to-do-in-tasmania/eco tourism-trail.

Hobart on Foot

o Hobart's suburbs are strung-out to the north and south along both shores of the Derwent River – but the city centre, waterfront, Battery Point and the North Hobart foodie strip are all entirely walkable.

o If you're only here for a few days, consider booking your accommodation somewhere central and seeing the city on foot instead of hiring a car. Parking in the city can be a drag, and the local bus network is available if you're exploring further afield.

Overtourism

Hobart has become a hugely popular tourism destination in recent years, coinciding (unsurprisingly) with the the arrival of MONA. But this has put huge pressure on the local housing market, with many property owners opting to cash-in on the weekend tourist market, rather than lease their houses to long-term local tenants. As a result, Hobart now has a homelessness problem, while accommodation prices for tourists are sky-high.

Dos & Don'ts

Although largely informal in their everyday dealings, Hobartians do observe some (unspoken) rules of etiquette.

Greetings Shake hands with men, women and children when meeting for the first time and when saying goodbye. Female friends are often greeted with a single kiss on the cheek.

Invitations If you're invited to someone's house for a BBQ or dinner, don't turn up empty handed: bring a bottle of wine or some beers.

Shouting No, not yelling. 'Shouting' at the bar means buying a round of drinks: if someone buys you one, don't leave without buying them one too.

To help combat this situation, consider travelling in the off season (any time other than summer), and booking your stay at an established hotel/B&B/hostel, rather than a short-term holiday rental house or apartment.

Safe Travel

o Hobart is just as safe as any other Australian capital city: common sense will get you by.

o Mt Wellington looks close enough to be a Hobart suburb, but the weather here can change rapidly. If you're bushwalking or biking, check the forecasts and be prepared for anything.

o Hobart has always been a hard-drinking town: late night on the waterfront can get unpleasant.

COVID-19 & Hobart

o Tasmania's response to Covid-19 has been rigorous and very successful. Tight border controls, swift lockdown protocols, strict quarantine for returning travellers, solid state-wide communication and public adherence to social distancing and hygiene guidelines have all helped.

o At the time of writing, despite the Delta variant having an impact nationally, vaccine rollouts were bringing rays of cautious optimism.

Toilets

o Toilets in Hobart are sit-down Western style.

o There aren't too many public toilets in central Hobart: try Salamanca Sq, or head into a pub.

o Alternatively, many parks and playgrounds around the suburbs have public toilets; see www.toiletmap.gov.au for locations.

Tourist Information

Hobart Visitor Information Centre
(☏ 03-6238 4222; www.hobarttravelcentre.com.au; 20 Davey St; ⏲ 8.30am-5pm Mon-Fri, from 9am Sat & Sun) Poised perfectly between the CBD and the waterfront. Information, maps and state-wide tour, transport and accommodation bookings.

Hobart City Council

(☎ 03-6238 2711; www.
hobartcity.com.au; 16
Elizabeth St; ☺ 8.15am-
5.15pm Mon-Fri) City-
council information:
parks, transport,
events and recreation.

Parks & Wildlife Service

(☎ 1300 135
513; www.parks.tas.gov.au;
134 Macquarie St, Hobart;
☺ 9am-5pm Mon-Fri) For
national parks info;
inside the Service
Tasmania office.

Wilderness Society Office

(☎ 03-6281 1910;
www.wilderness.org.au;
130 Davey St, Hobart;
☺ 9am-5pm Mon-Fri)
Info on conservation in
Tasmania's wilderness
areas.

Discover Tasmania

(www.discover
tasmania.com.au) A
statewide, catch-all
info repository.

Visas

All visitors to Australia,
and thus Tasmania,
need a visa. Apply
online through the
Department of Immi-
gration & Border Pro-
tection (www.border.
gov.au).

eVisitor (651)

o Many European
passport holders are
eligible for a free eVisitor
visa, allowing stays
in Australia for up to
three months within a
12-month period.

o eVisitor visas must
be applied for online.
They are electronically
stored and linked to
individual passport
numbers, so no stamp
in your passport is
required.

o It's advisable to apply
at least 14 days prior to
the proposed date of
travel to Australia.

Electronic Travel Authority (ETA; 601)

o Passport holders
from the European
countries eligible for
eVisitor visas, plus
passport holders from
Brunei, Canada, Hong
Kong, Japan, Malaysia,
Singapore, South Korea
and the USA, can apply
for either a visitor ETA
or business ETA.

o ETAs are valid for 12
months, with stays of
up to three months on
each visit.

o ETA visas cost $20.

Behind the Scenes

Send Us Your Feedback

We love to hear from travellers – your comments help make our books better. We read every word, and we guarantee that your feedback goes straight to the authors. Visit **lonelyplanet.com/contact** to submit your updates and suggestions.

Note: We may edit, reproduce and incorporate your comments in Lonely Planet products such as guidebooks, websites and digital products, so let us know if you don't want your comments reproduced or your name acknowledged. For a copy of our privacy policy visit lonelyplanet.com/privacy.

Charles' Thanks

Huge thanks to Amy for the gig, and to all the helpful souls I met on the road in Tasmania who flew through my questions with the greatest of ease. Biggest thanks of all to Meg, who held the increasingly chaotic fort while I was busy scooting around in the sunshine – and made sure that the kids were fed, watered, schooled, tucked-in and read-to.

Acknowledgements

Climate map data adapted from Peel MC, Finlayson BL & McMahon TA (2007) 'Updated World Map of the Köppen-Geiger Climate Classification', Hydrology and Earth System Sciences, 11, 163344.

Front cover photograph: View from kunanyi/Mt Wellington; Darren Tierney/ Shutterstock ©

Back cover photograph: Cray fishing boats, Hobart; Albert Pego/ Shutterstock ©

This Book

This 2nd edition of Lonely Planet's *Pocket Hobart* guidebook was researched and written by Charles Rawlings-Way.

This guidebook was produced by:

Senior Product Editors
Amy Lynch, Tasmin Waby

Product Editors
Hannah Cartmel, Claire Rourke

Senior Cartographer
Valentina Kremenchutskaya, Julie Sheridan

Book & Cover Designer
Fergal Condon

Assisting Editors
Bruce Evans, Clare Healy, Catherine Naghten, Kathryn Rowan, Saralinda Turner

Thanks to
Jennifer Carey, Ian Cartmel, Daniel Corbett, Joel Cotterell, Melanie Dankel, Liz Heynes, Harsha Maheshwari, Claire Naylor, Rachel Rawling, Tracy Whitmey, Polly Whittington

Index

See also separate subindexes for:

- ⊗ **Eating p155**
- ⊙ **Drinking p156**
- ✪ **Entertainment p157**
- ⬡ **Shopping p157**

Sights 000

Map Pages **000**

🍴 Eating

Our Writer

Charles Rawlings-Way

Charles is a tireless travel writer who has penned 40-something titles for Lonely Planet – including guides to Singapore, Toronto, Sydney, Tasmania, New Zealand, the South Pacific and Australia – and numerous articles. After dabbling in the dark arts of architecture, cartography, project management and busking, Charles hit the road for Lonley Planet in 2005 and hasn't stopped travelling since.

Published by Lonely Planet Global Limited
CRN 554153
2nd edition – March 2022
ISBN 978 1 78701390 2
© Lonely Planet 2022   Photographs © as indicated 2022
10 9 8 7 6 5 4 3 2 1
Printed in Singapore